A. H Tevis

Beyond the Sierras

Observations on the Pacific Coast

A. H Tevis

Beyond the Sierras
Observations on the Pacific Coast

ISBN/EAN: 9783743317611

Manufactured in Europe, USA, Canada, Australia, Japa

Cover: Foto ©ninafisch / pixelio.de

Manufactured and distributed by brebook publishing software (www.brebook.com)

A. H Tevis

Beyond the Sierras

BEYOND THE SIERRAS;

OR,

OBSERVATIONS ON THE PACIFIC COAST.

BY

REV. A. H. TEVIS, A.M., D.D.,
AUTHOR OF "JESUITISM, THE BIBLE, AND THE SCHOOLS."

> "A wide domain of mysteries
> And signs that men misunderstand!
> A land of space and dreams; a land
> Of sea-salt lakes and dried-up seas!
> A land of caves and caravans,
> And lonely wells and pools."
> —JOAQUIN MILLER.

PHILADELPHIA:
J. B. LIPPINCOTT & CO.,
1877.

Copyright, 1877, by J. B. LIPPINCOTT & CO.

TO
THE MEMORY OF
HON. WIRT HOPKINS,
LATE ASSAYER U. S. MINT, CARSON CITY, NEVADA,
ONE OF THE BEST FRIENDS EARTH EVER GAVE ME,
WHOSE HAND PENNED SOME OF THESE PAGES,
AND WHOSE MANLY HEART, COMMON SENSE,
AND PERSONAL FAVORS SHOWN ME AND MINE,
WILL NEVER BE FORGOTTEN WHILE LIFE LASTS,
THIS VOLUME
IS FAITHFULLY DEDICATED.

PREFATORY.

THIS volume is presented to the reader, not claiming any profundity or very rare features, but as an answer, somewhat, to the numerous inquiries that have been made of me regarding the Pacific Coast.

The climate, the hard times, and the overcrowded population of the Eastern States have turned the thoughts of thousands toward this part of the United States. Here the climate is near perfection, times are easier than in the East, and the population is not crowded, hence this country may well claim the attention of the people. But California is not Paradise; it has its delights, it is true, but it certainly has its objections,—some of which have been alluded to in the following pages. It has been my design to give such information as I have found by experience that a person wants when he arrives on these shores. Of course, this book does not "contain it all," but it does contain such as I could get in the time allotted. I do not beg mercy for this volume,—" what is writ is writ." Silly critics need not be feared, and sensible ones are always charitable.

I am under obligations to the late Hon. Wirt Hopkins, A.M., for many suggestions, as well as for some of the pages contained in this book. Had not death taken him away, this volume would have possessed additional interest, for he would have contributed very largely to its pages. A residence of a quarter of a century on this coast and his literary ability well fitted him for the work.

Some of the accounts given of vegetable productions, etc., will seem like unfounded exaggerations. Many of them are exceptions, but they are given to show what can be done by one of the greatest countries the sun ever shone upon.

There is no doubt of the wonderful features of the Pacific Coast, but whether the reader will ever see or enjoy them must depend entirely upon himself. I would not utter a word to induce him to come; it is a question he must settle for himself.

A. H. T.

SAN FRANCISCO, CALIFORNIA, March 28, 1877.

CONTENTS.

CHAPTER		PAGE
I.	A REMOTE STATE	9
II.	"SHALL I GO TO THE PACIFIC COAST?"	16
III.	LOSS OR GAIN, WHY?	23
IV.	NATURE'S RETURNS TO THE HUSBANDMAN	34
V.	MINES AND MINING	42
VI.	A GARDEN IN A GARDEN	52
VII.	NORTH OF THE BAY	59
VIII.	A LAND OF MILK AND HONEY	70
IX.	A LAND OF MILK AND HONEY—CONTINUED	82
X.	SOCIAL LIFE	118
XI.	THE PEARL OF THE SIERRAS	131
XII.	SUMMERING AT LAKE TAHOE	138
XIII.	TOWARDS YOSEMITE	145
XIV.	YOSEMITE	165
XV.	INTERESTING PLACES AND THINGS	177
XVI.	A GLIMPSE AT THE "HEATHEN CHINEE"	184
XVII.	"HARD LINES" IN TRAVEL	194
XVIII.	INCIDENTS AND OBSERVATIONS IN ARIZONA	207
XIX.	MORAL AND INTELLECTUAL OUTLOOK	225
XX.	LOCALITIES AND BUSINESS	235
XXI.	SOME OBJECTIONS	244
XXII.	MY ASSOCIATE	253

BEYOND THE SIERRAS;
OR,
OBSERVATIONS ON THE PACIFIC COAST.

CHAPTER I.

A REMOTE STATE.

"You are not for obscurity designed."—DRYDEN.

It is a common saying that this is an age of such intellectual advancement that a cosmopolitan world is made a neighborly community. That really does very well for a sentence to weave into a florid Fourth-of-July speech, but does not contain facts, nor reliable information to a reasonable degree.

Science has made such advancement that, politically and commercially, nations are near each other. But lightning express trains, and rapid ocean travel and even telegraphy, and daily journals, rich with news, greeting us at early breakfast, do not always bring adjoining counties into very close acquaintanceship, much less remote

States and countries. We are blessed with much information that is quite reliable of all discovered parts of the world, while of the minutiæ of topography, geography, the social and intellectual character of the people, and a thousand and one other things of a given section, we may know but little.

We study self-interest much more than history or science, hence we are much better informed in matters that pertain to our individual benefit than the general condition of the world.

It is said Americans live close together in feelings and interests. This must be taken with a grain of allowance, for thousands care little or nothing and know nothing of men and things beyond their own door-yard.

The maps lay down a section of country of 200,000 square miles between the 32d and 42d parallels of latitude, and 114th and 124th degrees of longitude, and label it *California.*

The pupil at school is taught that it was and is yet, to a limited extent, "the land of gold," and that it is bounded on the west by the Pacific Ocean, and on other sides by certain States and a territory.

But of the State, and the whole Pacific slope—of the topography, climatic character, mineral wealth, agricultural features and advantages, isothermal influences, etc., comparatively little is known.

Invalids come to enjoy the climate, having heard

of it as a near relation to the early character of the Garden of Eden. Tourists, many of whom come as the result of a long desire to "take a trip," irrespective of information, rush hither and thither, "doing up" the entire coast in a few brief weeks, and, having an imperfect knowledge of everything, go home with overdrawn ideas, or else have information short of the facts.

A gentleman of New York—a lawyer of some prominence—once writing to me for information, said, " We know no more in detail of the Pacific coast than we do of some parts of Asia."

It seemed hyperbolical, yet no doubt was true. A professor in one of the leading universities of the West addressed the writer a letter in which he spoke of " Nevada *territory*," when the *State* had been organized at least thirteen years.

We do not say that persons are to be severely censured for the want of this knowledge, because it is impossible for any but an idiot to know everything, but it plainly indicates the lack of information concerning the Pacific coast. Though it be professors and professional men that so greatly err, we must not so much blame as assist, considering the subject.

The history of the entire extent of country west of the Rocky Mountains is a very interesting one.

The Great Salt Lake is to-day no doubt the remnant of one vast inland sea that originally covered thousands upon thousands of square miles.

The geological evidences in the ranges of mountains are of the most indubitable character, substantiating the theory of a sea once covering the waste lowlands of Utah and Eastern Nevada. In the highlands of the latter State there are evidences almost everywhere of volcanic action, which was no doubt the prime agent in shaping its present physical aspect.

Of California even stranger theories have been held. How curious that this State, with its mountains and fertile valleys, should ever have been called an island, whereas to-day there is but a poor evidence of it ever having been even a first-class peninsula!

There are evidences that the ocean once covered many places that are inland to-day, yet to our thinking there are poor indications that the State was entirely isolated by the waters of the sea. But such was the fact two hundred years ago, or at any rate such was the idea held at that not very remote period.

About two centuries ago, a history of America was written by one John Ogilby, in which he says, "We shall close up our discourse of these islands that lie north of the Equinoctial Line, with a discourse of California, especially so-called, which was by many thought and described to be a peninsula, or half island, by reason of the bay which divides it from Quivivian and New Gallacia towards the north, runneth much narrower than it doth southerly, which made them think that somewhere or other at the north it was joined to the main land of America. But later discoveries have found it to be a perfect island, and altogether separate from the continent. . . ."

This is a fact in connection with the history of California, if fact it is, that sounds strangely to many students of the geography of this coast.

California was of no special interest to the United States till after the close of the Mexican War, when it was ceded to our government by the terms of the treaty of peace. Even then by many statesmen it was thought to be of little value, save as a coast defence. Gold had not been discovered, the vast and incomparable resources of these rich plains had not been developed, and the beneficial effects of the climate had not been thought of.

But succeeding events, with which the reader is familiar, brought the coast prominently before the eye of the world, and in comparatively close relationship with the other territories and States. But the attention given has been mainly towards the leading features of the coast, rather than the minutiæ of the State. It is but little known that in almost every sense there is an essential difference between this and the other States of the Union,—

that in many of the habits and customs the people are unlike, while in the natural characteristics there is as great or greater dissimilarity.

How few, aside from those that have lived or visited here, have a proper idea of the natural advantages, climate, soil, and the artificial developments that are enjoyed in this land of bright sunshine and gold. It is not known by the masses that here can be found all the climates of the known world, while almost everything the world produces can be found within the limits of the State.

California is "part and parcel" of the great sisterhood of States; but it is not felt and realized like in the States of the East, unless it be by the politicians of the coast, whose philanthropy makes them desire to "serve" the country for their country's good. And we doubt if they feel any very great amount of patriotism prompting them at times. It is so far away from the seat of government in the East, and from the various matters that stir and interest the people of other States, that the feelings of relationship and sympathy are comparatively weakened. As much of the spirit of loyalty, perhaps, prevails here as in the average State if it were aroused. But distance and relative isolation have dulled the keen interest that is felt in the various localities of the East. Business, aims, ambition, feelings, sympathies, thoughts are greatly localized in this country, and are directed to developments that pertain alone to this coast.

Hundreds of miles intervene between the great family of the body politic in the Atlantic States and the relatively small branch on the Pacific; and the pulsations of sympathetic life are kept in motion by a few telegraph wires and a single railroad, which public highway has no more feelings in common with the interests of the East or West, aside from the aggrandizement of their own "ring," than they have with the development of the sugar plantations of Louisiana. And then, geographical lines and topographical features add to the *felt* idea, so to speak, of the remoteness. Does not this State lie on a far-off and relatively unknown coast? And does it not retain yet in the hearts of its native population a feeling of at least interest in the land where it used to belong—Mexico? And are there not great mountain chains, whose summits reach into the everlasting snows, that lie between this State and the interests and associations of the East? And do not these add to the idea of remoteness that is felt by all?

These are the very barriers that prevent many from moving to this coast, whose greatest desire is to find a land of such delightful climate and incomparable resources as California.

CHAPTER II.

"SHALL I GO TO THE PACIFIC COAST?"

"Let the end try the man."—SHAKSPEARE.

In answering this oft-repeated question, I shall endeavor to be concise, and at the same time definite.

First, if a poor man, and you can make a living at home, stay there. The reasons for this are many, all of which need not be mentioned to reveal the philosophy of the advice given. The immense mineral resources of the coast are mostly in the hands of the moneyed few, and nearly nothing is left for individual exertion, as in the palmy days of the "gold excitement."

It is somewhat so with agriculture. Although there are immense tracts of government land unoccupied, the scarcity of water, difficulty of access, and other causes, render not a small amount of capital absolutely necessary to enable a man to bring such land under cultivation.

The same is true in very many branches of business to a degree. The expenses of living in certain remote sections are much greater than in the East; and, by the way, in some places not very remote, too. And although the major part of our population to-day earn their living by their daily toil, it is very frequently next to impossible for a stranger from east of the Rocky Mountains, unless he have friends to help him, to obtain employment of any kind immediately.

The reason for this is plain. The methods of doing business are so entirely different, and the kinds of work so new, that a new-comer can hardly earn his board for his employer. Consequently, it is best not to hastily, nor unthoughtedly, follow the advice of the late Horace Greeley, and " go west." It is a long ways from the East to California, and many things are met that are not pleasant or lucrative. If you are determined, and have will sufficient to stem the tide of the various opposing elements that will meet you, you will be safe in coming to the Pacific.

There is no doubt that if, with these qualities, a man have a small amount of ready money, and goes into any branch of business with which he is acquainted and to which he is adapted, and will keep a modicum of the frugality and economy supposed to have been taught him in his youth, a reasonable success is about as certain as taxation.

In all lines of trade on this coast the old proverb, " He who by the plough would thrive," etc., holds true in every instance. *A man must work,* either with hands or brain, and if with both, so much the better. Drones never thrive in the West.

Instances by the thousand could be given to the point where men, with very little money, have in a few years accumulated a competency, if not wealth, and I cannot recall a single instance of a failure unless there were good causes, such as drunkenness, laziness, or a propensity for some species of gambling.

This does not apply to any one branch of business alone, but to all alike; pre-supposing, of course, that a man will not undertake or engage in anything of which he has not at least a little knowledge, if not experience.

And here it is well to state that a cause of serious trouble to many has been a desire to engage in some line of business of which they knew nothing whatever. A personal friend of the writer, who was a fine mechanic, and who had capital enough to have given him a good start in his legitimate business, after arriving, said he " did not come to California to work at the bench or retail his merchandise." He went into the drug business, and at the end of the first year he was able to sell out his stock with the loss of half his capital. He then went into the manufacture of matches, which in less than a year brought him to the position meant by that significant word "broke." With no money, he came down to first principles, went to work at his trade, and is now a wealthy wholesale dealer in New York City.

Whatever talent Providence may have endowed you with, it is best to cultivate that, and not rush after the impossible until you can financially afford it, for education, even that of experience, costs money here. For instance, if you were of the farm "to the manor born," it is best to remain one until independence shall have been achieved in that vocation.

Every one in starting for the Pacific coast should make certain resolutions that are as unalterable as the laws of the Medes and Persians. First, never touch spirituous liquors. Leave drinking to the pioneers of '49, many of whose throats have become case-hardened. Remember the bane of California is wine- and brandy-drinking. Millions of gallons of intoxicating liquors are manufactured every year, and millions and millions of money are squandered by drink. You cannot compromise with this habit here and remain temperate and fortunate.

Do not try to beat a professional gambler out of his coin. You will not succeed, even if he seem to be drunk, for he never is. Live by all means economically, and whatever may be your receipts, try to save part of them. Fully make up your mind before starting what you intend to engage in, and then do that and nothing else. Vacillation is expensive.

This work is intended to afford reliable information, sufficient for your direction, in selecting a location for a home. Above all, unless wealthy, let mining enterprises of all kinds alone, for it is far better to let millionaires draw the blanks, and they are legion in comparison with the prizes.

One great cause of disappointment to the immigrant is a wrong idea, fostered by articles written by land-sharks and others who are financially interested in encouraging immigration, giving false, or at least overdrawn accounts of the chances and facilities for making money enjoyed by residents of the Pacific coast.

We would not, upon the other hand, discourage any one, nor depreciate the facilities and chances in this country. There are good opportunities, and very much that is charming, but each man, as a rule, should be his own adviser and agent in all financial matters, so far as financial speculations are concerned. This book is not written in the interest of any speculator or real estate manipulator. We have, in some instances, given statements that seem to be highly colored, if not incredible. But we have given them because *they are facts*, and show what the country is capable of doing.

The truth is, that here the same energy is required, and the same industry essential, as in other parts of the world. And, indeed, I am inclined to think it requires more, for here it is either success or failure financially. This portion of the world has steep hills, and a man on the down track moves very rapidly. A medium in prosperity or adversity is not the rule, we are inclined to think.

A strong point in favor of California is, that a competency is gained, if gained at all, before old age has destroyed the faculty for enjoying the fruits of one's labor.

I have not yet heard of a case of any man who understood the business in which he was engaged, and followed it for five or six years, starting free from debt, who did not become independent in all cases except mining, which is an exceedingly *illegitimate* legitimate business. Debts are ruinous, particularly from the high rate of interest, which, with the best security (real estate), ranges, according to the locality, from one to three per cent. per month.

No man should entertain the thought for a moment of starting in business on borrowed capital, unless he entertains the unfortunate idea that "he has nothing to lose and all to gain." It may at least prove very unfortunate to the person of whom he borrows the capital. Better, by far, for his own personal feelings, his credit, his family, his all, to start in some humble business, and work his way up on capital that he knows *is his own*.

It may be said to all in general, but agriculturists in particular, that there is plenty of room, as may be seen by reference to the account given of San Bernardino County alone. Land monopolists are in the way of immigration, but these will of necessity yield to the pressure as time rolls on, and their vast possessions will be subdivided. Land is abundant and of the best quality. There are a limited number of machine-shops and factories for the mechanic, rivers and bays for the sailor, and unlimited underground workings for the miner. There is also a laborious and ripe field for the minister, and unlimited number of children for the teacher, and quibblings and crime to be settled by the lawyer, and sickness, notwithstanding the wonderful climate, to be cured or increased by the physician.

CHAPTER III.

LOSS OR GAIN, WHY?

"No help nor hope nor view had I, nor person to befriend me,
So I must toil and sweat and broil and labor to sustain me;
To plough and sow, to reap and mow, my father bred me early;
For one, he said, to labor bred, was a match for fortune fairly."

We have our adaptations in mental ballast, physical strength, moral force, financial ability, etc. By these is the determination to triumph made absolutely successful. Success in the broadest acceptation of the term depends upon these possessions. Laws of adaptation run through all the woof and web of human experience. You may denominate it a divine "call," as that held by the orthodox ministry. Why not? It does no injustice to man or dishonor to God, surely. The ministry, doubtless, saves more souls, but certainly does not fill a greater area in God's plan than the conscientious farmer or honest laborer. Adaptation is the great desideratum after all, and the really successful man cannot eliminate any of the elements mentioned in the beginning of this chapter. The Rothschilds have been but partially successful, because they have succeeded only in finances. But they have grandly succeeded there, because adapted to financial manipulations. A. T. Stewart made a successful merchant, but mayhap he would have failed as a farmer. This is a diversified world. Various temperaments, various climates, various causes, having their various effects, are observed everywhere, and wise is he who joins affinities.

Thousands have been lured to these shores by the glowing accounts given of this country, while thousands of others, because of adverse circumstances rendering it impossible for them to come, have

"Sat and gazed and wondered"

in a spirit of bitter disappointment, because they, too, could not come. Many have been fortunate in not being able to come, and many unfortunate because they are here.

All changes should be made with reference to some legitimate end; never change for change sake. True, it is said that "change of pasture fattens cattle," but it is the *pasture* that gives the increase, and not the mere *change*. Change sometimes takes from close provender to no provender at all.

Thousands utterly fail in this country, and go back eastward breathing out anathemas against the country and people, not because there was nothing worth gaining, but because they never had a well-defined idea of what they wanted to gain, or any adaptation for the special means of livelihood that chance to be open.

We have already intimated that under certain conditions some need hardly expect success on the Pacific coast until there shall have been a radical change in the ways of business and rules of society. That there is a great deal of quasi honesty no one will deny. And to intensify the idea, and say that there is a great deal of first-class stealing, yet under legitimate names, is but stating a well-known fact. Yet notwithstanding this, it is entirely safe to say that business principles more strictly govern commercial transactions here than anywhere else in the United States. Promptness, energy, economy, and frankness are essential characteristics in successful, legitimate business. And this is the only kind of business that should be desired.

This part of the great sisterhood of States is to a degree isolated from the rest of the country, so that California is an *imperium in imperio*.

This very fact of isolation by a great distance from "the States" has been a means of selecting those that have sought the Pacific coast as a permanent home or field for business. A peculiar class of people are here, and have been from the discovery of gold in 1848. The Mexican War had taken from their homes in the East men of all classes and grades, but men of strong physique and nerve, having metal of which heroes are made, for war calls out the nation's most valorous men, albeit they are sometimes men of bad hearts and abandoned lives. Such was the character of many of the men that rushed against the land of Montezuma in 1846. The treaty of peace with Mexico threw upon the country a band of men made adventurers by nature or their experience in the war. They were without employment, and many had no desire to return to their native country. Hence, attracted by the new country that had just been ceded to the government, many drifted to California to be participants in the exciting scenes that followed.

Adventurers are made of good material; they may sometimes be warped and angular in character, but, if properly controlled, make the best of citizens. The influx of immigration from '48 to '52, and to a great degree in succeeding years, was composed of this class of men.

Drones, as a rule, are not the stirring, go-ahead, valorous men that conquer and utilize the world's outposts. This adventurous class of men have given a character to the whole Pacific coast that is world-wide, and that will continue through many decades. Who does not know that Californians are noted for their energy and enterprise?

Foss's celebrated stage-drives to the Geysers, whose break-neck speed hundreds will remember, was in a staging way what the whole population do in a commercial line. Fortunes have been made and squandered, leaving the possessor penniless, in a week.

The great distance of California from the Eastern States, where the controlling men were to come from, the hazardous journey, and the great dangers attending it, were barriers against all except such as had strong mental and physical endowments. And the very same, to a slight degree, yet culls the class that comes to this coast.

It is not making an overdrawn statement to say that the highest order of intelligence is to be found on the Pacific coast. There is more universality of education among the people than in any considerable part of the United States. Hence the success that is seen everywhere. Money, as we have already indicated, is not picked up anywhere, but is secured by intelligent efforts.

It is readily seen why many succeed and many fail in this country. The faint-hearted young man, whose idea of happiness is to be found in the immediate neighborhood that gave him birth, will soon learn that he is ill-adapted to the hurly-burly of California.

Mother's affection should ever be cherished;

she is the best and dearest one on earth. But it must be remembered that if the extreme West is sought as a future home, her apron-strings do not span the mountains and plains that intervene. Many a man, good and true, to my knowledge, has most signally failed because he could not practically sever himself from home, and leap strong and unfettered upon the stage of success.

Will and spirit are worth more than money here. With them you may be penniless and acquire a fortune, but without them your wealth goes, never to return.

If men lack success here, in nine cases out of ten it is because they lack adaptation.

Positiveness is among the first necessary articles, then, if you haven't money; but little matter, if you have will and energy. Money is here in sufficient abundance for every one that comes, if he but seek it properly.

There is great diversity in California; this has reference to the gifts of Nature as well as human character. Hence success depends largely upon manipulations with reference to these diversities. Even energy and brains *ad libitum* will not extract a fortune from a barren desert.

A clearly defined idea of the end to be gained should always lie at the very beginning of the journey to this coast. "Never go it blind," if you would succeed, is an old adage, and never had more force than here. Make up your mind distinctly what you expect to do when you shall have arrived, then be governed only by the circumstances that bear upon your desired occupation.

The nature of the climate must be considered, for climate is as varied almost as landscapes or a native's word. If you be, or intend to be, a farmer, the soil must be your temporary theme at least. Nature has thrown a goodly garb over all the land, but, "mark well," do not trust to appearances. Invest cautiously; a thousand will entice you; prospects the most inviting will unfold before you; and if you have been a matter-of-fact, domestic kind of a man, the tendency will be to invest, and "make a corner" on all the opportunities, or a sufficient number of them to entirely "corner" you. Perhaps, of all places, more calm, steady thought is required here.

No land, to a given number of acres, produces more abundantly than California. But agricultural pursuits require more thoughtfulness here than anywhere else. A successful farmer in this country would, if he were to farm on the same principles he does in the States, make a lamentable failure. The proper time, if used, and the right kind and amount of labor, are sure to bloom out in an abundant harvest.

A young man, without money or capital, save

his own will and nerve, hired some land, borrowed money from his landlord to buy grain, and put in his crop. It was an auspicious time and a favorable year. So promising was the harvest that the landlord cancelled the debt for borrowed money, and gave the young man fifteen hundred dollars in ready cash for his claim. This was an amount of money very respectable, when it is remembered that it was made without any capital being invested, and not to exceed perhaps two months' actual labor.

This must not be permitted to allure any young man to attempt a trip across the continent expecting a like success; it might not be found. Like opportunities *may* be found, but they are not now, nor have they ever been, the rule.

Financial failures are of almost daily occurrence in California. But while there are failures, and many that do no more than make a livelihood, there is no doubt but more money can be made here with less labor and money, if both be judiciously invested, than in any other State in the Union.

Many lose their spirit upon arriving, and droop like a wounded bird, unable to rise above even the petty barriers that interpose, and finally that eminently unpleasant yet rarely fatal disease, *nostalgia*, carries the disappointed one beyond the mountains eastwards "to the familiar scenes of the long ago."

Nine out of ten expect to see no difference on this coast from the scenes of the East, save perhaps strange faces. What a mistake! Go to France. Stand in the Champs Elysées, or hover around the Tuileries, or promenade the day long the city boulevards. Cross down to Italy. Visit Rome, walk the Appian Way, but debar from the thoughts and eye historic interest and the surrounding European evidences, and yet you will not feel the change more sensibly, save a little more—and only a little more—of the foreign tongue. Go to London, and, save the places of history that would surround you, you would not be more sensibly impressed with the change than you are in the metropolis of this coast from the scenes of your childhood's home—and manhood's, too, for that matter—in the East.

You may have felt the financial burden in coming. The vast majority do. It was evident that you felt hampered in the East, else you would not have come. Even one first-class fare, including etceteras, is not a little matter, to be played with as a toy. Long before you have reached your destination you have unmistakably marked the decrease of your money and a tremendous increase in prices of everything you purchase. The morning newspaper that you purchased at home for not to exceed five pennies you now get for twice or thrice or four times that amount. But consolation is somewhat restored with the thought that "I need not buy these articles." But eat you must,—and at a price two or three times the expense at home.

This is *en route*. When you arrive, living is cheap,—even cheaper than a corresponding living East,—but different money is required from what you have been using. That which you have always used as ready money no longer passes, and you sell the diminishing pile at, it seems to you, a heavy discount. For gold and silver alone pass here,—or, rather, we should say gold, because even silver is frequently discounted.

Here you learn the uses—for the first time, it may be—of the memorable "bit," whose value is as adjustable as many of the conveniences you have to deal with.

You go shopping (you have learned that a "bit" is really twelve and a half cents); you buy a bit's worth, for instance; you can't make the change, of course, for who ever heard of pennies in California commerce? Twenty-five cents is tendered and a dime given back as change. You at once feel that you have lost two cents and a half. It is not the loss especially that hurts, but the principle of taking what is not even asked that goads.

You learn that that is the ordinary way of dealing, and you at once feel that you are in a land of financial sharps and in danger of being "fleeced."

This is a rule in ordinary traffic all over the entire coast, and is not so greatly disliked when it is once understood and "the rule begins to work both ways,"—that is, *you* take the "long bit" for twelve and a half cents, as others have done from you.

But the peculiar notions of small change on the Pacific coast have certainly been of no special advantage to the masses, but an absolute disadvantage.

The habit of refusing pennies, five-cent pieces, dimes, and, in better times, quarters, sprung from the "good old days" when every man felt rich even if he was not absolutely so. The custom might sometimes be practicable, but certainly has not been the best for the country.

It may sometimes be unpopular to take or give your small change, but certainly it is neither unmanly nor unjust. Even California would doubtless have been better off if she had in every respect have lived a little more in the United States. These very customs that we have alluded to regarding small things have helped discourage many a man, and assisted in his failure. Let me see, don't we get the idea somewhere of battles lost or won in ancient times just by the peculiar indications of the flight of birds? It was a small matter, but it had its effect. So of these little things, just at a time when the spirit is sensitive and discouraged by the strangeness of its surroundings. Economy, of course, is the first law in success here as well as elsewhere. And it can be practised very rigidly if one desires. Fashion has not such an iron grasp upon men as in the East. It is in perfect order to wear anything that is decent, and to eat anything that is healthful and life-sustaining. Domestic expenses need not be great,— provisions are not expensive, and some of them are very cheap. Everything you have will bring money, and a good price. The market is always open.

CHAPTER IV.

NATURE'S RETURNS TO THE HUSBANDMAN.

"Do not smile at me, that I cast her off,
For thou shalt find she will outstrip all praise,
And make it halt behind her."—SHAKSPEARE.

A VOLUME lies before us for this chapter, if we would but collect the material for it. For who could write of the incredulous productions of this State without filling a volume, if he were to tell it all? To write less than the truth, when one can give the facts, is to reveal unmistakable evidence of cowardice; while to write facts as they are, is certain to call upon one's self the charge of lacking veracity.

And it were not so difficult if the reader and the writer could look only at one locality, and there find what we hope to condense in these few pages. But such cannot be done and do justice to the greatest country yet discovered on earth. Here are nearly 200,000 square miles of wonders, and vegetable and mineral wealth, lying all the way, too, from the regions of perpetual snow to the regions below the level of the sea, and on a horizontal plane from north of Mount Shasta to near the Gulf of California. And it might be added, that the area extends to the frozen shores of Alaska. And yet, of the treasures lying north of the south line of Oregon this chapter has but little to do; enough troops up in array before us to subdivide into sections.

From the time you leave the snow line, near "Cape Horn," on the Central Pacific Railroad, or step from the steamer in San Francisco Bay, you enter the domains of one continuous garden the year round. While the Eastern States are locked in the embrace of winter, and you travel from New York to the eastern line of this State in furs and wraps, these farmers are sowing their grain and planting seeds that will produce a harvest incredible in magnitude. These January days, as the mercury revels among the zeros almost anywhere in the East, miles upon miles of fields of wheat are being sown, that in a few months will make a golden covering for tens of thousands of acres.

The people of the East have a very incorrect idea of the magnitude and manner of farming in this country. Wheat is now, and will be for all time to come, perhaps, the great staple product. Already it is shipped to the Eastern States, Europe, Asia, Australia, and other countries, and nearly all the islands of the sea. There is hardly a doubt but California can itself produce enough of this article to subsist the present population of the United States.

In the last six months there have been shipped to San Francisco alone 9,541,000 quintals of wheat. This would be equivalent to 15,901,700 bushels, nearly. As this was a six months' shipment only, we may reasonably suppose that the amount would be doubled in the year, making 31,803,400 bushels to that one market. Now take into consideration home consumption, and the amount shipped from other points, and the aggregate becomes enormous. There are now, while I write (January), in the port of San Francisco, under engagement to load, twenty-five vessels, representing 34,400 tons of tonnage, with a carrying capacity of 1,000,000 quintals.

There was shipped from Oregon, independent

of home consumption, in the year 1876, 2,894,722 quintals of wheat, amounting to nearly five million bushels. This was valued at nearly five millions of dollars, and was a gain of three-quarters of a million in value in a twelvemonth. This is from an area of country not one-fifth as large as the wheat-growing portion of California.

At the risk of wearying the reader, I shall give a very brief idea of the way of farming, for the wheat farms are sometimes very great, and it is thought frequently in the East to be impossible to farm on such gigantic principles; for farmers here sometimes have thousands of acres in wheat alone. I heard of one farmer who had forty thousand acres of wheat sown. I cannot vouch for that; I did not see the farmer or his farm.

I did travel forty-odd miles by stage line, through one continuous body of wheat, in the San Joaquin Valley (pronounced San Wau-keen'). Of course, this belonged to several men.

As soon as the rainy season begins, say in October or November, the farmers begin their ploughing and sowing. Great numbers of teams are set to work, generally with the gang-plough, and almost immediately numbers of men begin sowing the grain, all by machinery. This is kept up month after month, or until the farmer has his desired amount of wheat sown. There is no cold weather to hinder him, and generally not rain storm severe enough to retard him. If he desires, he can sow continuously from November till May.

The dry weather begins about the first of May, giving a delightful season for the wheat to ripen, which it does as gradually as it is sown. The wheat is harvested very differently from what it is in the East. No dew to bother, and the storms are hidden months away in the distance. Reapers, in number proportionate to the magnitude of the harvest, are set to work. Instead of reapers, headers are often used,—a machine that is adjusted so as to clip off the heads of the wheat, thus saving a vast amount of labor in not handling the straw. When these are used, the wheat is often threshed at once and the grain sacked.

The wheat is threshed without binding or stacking, as in the East, save in limited quantities, the grain being forked up like loose hay.

When threshed and sacked, it is often ricked up and left lying in the field for months. These ricks of wheat are sometimes enormous. When Vallejo was a greater shipping point than now, sometimes there were miles of ricks of wheat waiting shipment.

Wheat has been known to yield one hundred and fifty bushels to the acre. This amount, of course, is rare. A friend of mine gathered 23,000 bushels of barley from 285 acres near San Pablo. California wheat is noted in all the markets of the world for its fine quality, and requires a great deal less labor to raise it, and is much more certain of a bountiful harvest, than in the Eastern States.

Illinois ranks next to California in the growth of wheat, but owing to the damp weather, etc., the harvest is not so certain.

This is not a corn-growing State, and yet some parts of California are being planted in corn with very fine success. Los Angeles County and parts of Santa Barbara and San Bernardino Counties are being developed as very fine corn-growing sections, —equalling the Middle or Western States. In some places irrigation is not even required. I have seen good corn growing at Santa Barbara with no irrigation but the fogs that roll in from the sea during the night.

In San Bernardino County, near the town of that name, eighty acres of corn, averaging one hundred and fifty bushels to the acre, and the ears so high that a man could not reach them standing on the ground, were raised entirely without artificial irrigation. Corn could be cultivated very successfully in many parts of the State if it were possible to furnish a sufficient amount of irrigation.

Almost all kinds of vegetables yield enormously, and a frugal, industrious husbandman can reap large profits.

Potatoes are one of the main products of California. They can be raised, too, where many other vegetables do not grow well. The amount produced during the past year (1876) was not up to the average amount, yet was certainly very great in the aggregate. There were shipped to San Francisco during that year 765,895 sacks, or about 76,589,500 pounds, or near 1,531,790 bushels. This will indicate to the reader something near the amount produced. Nearly or quite a thousand acres, each, are raised by many farmers. This part of agricultural life requires less labor than some others, and is quite remunerative, for the average yield is always fair, and a good market always sure.

Perhaps there is no department of agriculture that pays so well for the amount of money invested as a vegetable garden. The productions are very great, and the market always good.. Onions are very prolific, and grow very large, with little labor. Sometimes they grow to be eight inches in diameter.

Peanuts, in certain localities, are raised easily and produce prodigiously, and the market is always good. Pumpkins, especially in the southern part of the State, are very productive. Sometimes, and not unfrequently, the yield is so great that one can walk over a field stepping alone on the pumpkins. I knew of an instance where a gentleman paid the price of his land—one hundred dollars per acre—

the first year by the product of pumpkins which he raised on it, and that, too, without any more labor than ploughing the ground and planting the seeds. This fruit finds a ready sale, and will keep in some sections the year round. I saw pumpkins at Santa Barbara more than a year old. Tomatoes live in the open fields for several years. I have seen them four years old. And this fruit, fresh and luscious, can be had every month in the year. I have seen beets as long as a man. They are very profitable, being used not only for the table but for feeding cattle and the manufacture of sugar.

Strawberries are very profitable,—as much so as any of the productions of the garden. Think of it! yielding every month in the year. This January day they adorn many a table and gladden many a heart. And not your little, dwarfed kind, that look as if they were ashamed they ever came into the world, but large, plump ones, redder than a maiden's lips. Think of strawberries six inches in circumference! And yet such are not so unfrequent as you would think. Fine, scarlet, tempting ones can be had on this very wintry day, and that, too, fresh from the vines. Let me point to one instance. Out from Santa Cruz about six miles now can be seen a fine, tempting patch growing in the open air. The owner of the ranch says he can at any day or month of the year go into the patch and gather at least twenty quarts of these luscious berries in a short time. He has three thousand vines in cultivation, which occupy half an acre of ground, and from these he gathered during the past year six thousand quarts of the large crimson beauties. Half of this quantity he sold in the local markets at twenty cents per quart. Blossoms, green and flaming red ripe strawberries smile and look sedate, and blush side by side the whole year through on the same vine.

Does such a crop pay? They are not as much trouble to cultivate as a patch of string-beans would be; then, at an average of twenty cents a quart, the half-acre would net six hundred dollars per year.

CHAPTER V.

MINES AND MINING.

"Wealth heaped on wealth, nor truth nor safety buys,
The dangers gather as the treasures rise."
  Dr. Johnson.

In a previous chapter I perhaps may have appeared to speak too disparagingly of mines and mining enterprise. The only reason for this is the fact that mining is speculating, and speculations are always uncertain.

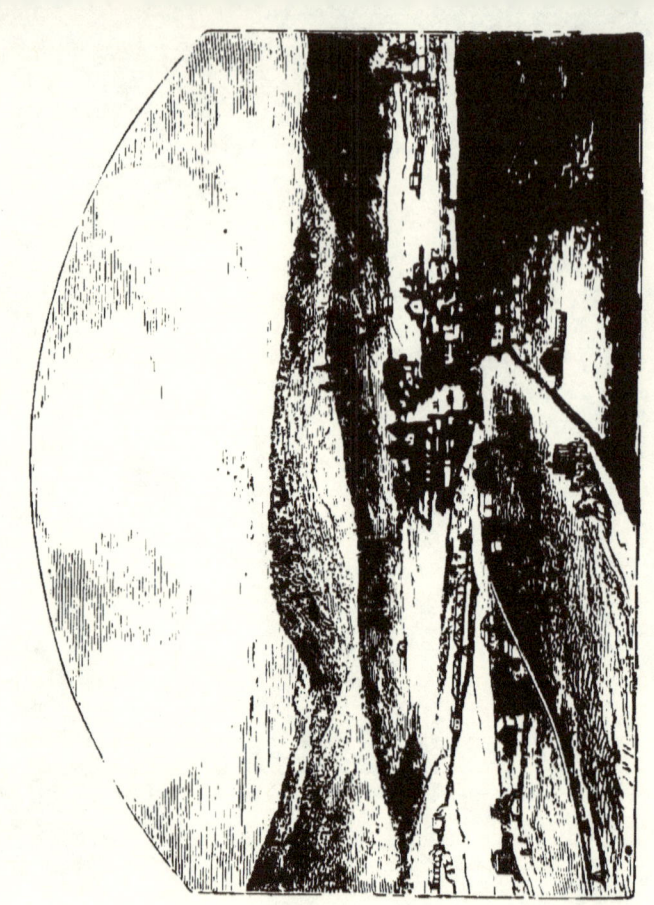

SUTTER'S CAMP, WHERE GOLD WAS DISCOVERED.

But it is a well-known fact that the unprecedentedly rapid development and subsequent growth of this country were brought about by our mines. Also, that the very backbone of the existence of Nevada, and to a great extent of California as well, is the possession of unlimited mineral resources.

It is hardly worth while in a work of this kind to attempt to give more than an outline of the progress of mining, from the finding of the fifty-cent "chispa," at Coloma, in California, by Marshall, to the present day of "Bonanzas" and wildcat stocks.

The first mining on this coast, as is well known, was for gold alone, and that in the most crude and simple manner: first by the "cradle or rocker," then the enormous improvement of the "long Tom," and finally with "sluices," which, on a large scale, is the method of to-day for working "placer" mines. The first comers merely worked the richest bars on the rivers, or the mere beds of ravines, and that in the most superficial manner, apparently satisfied with the cream alone, so to speak.

Hydraulic mining has at present almost entirely taken the place of all other methods of working surface diggings. This manner of washing was first introduced by Edward E. Matteson, at American Hill, Nevada County, California, in the year 1852, and, from his success, it soon became a very prominent feature of our mining undertakings.

The "sine qua non" in hydraulic working is fall for the water sufficient to give the requisite force, say from eighty to two hundred feet perpendicular. A hose of great strength is then prepared, from ten inches in diameter upwards, which carries the water into a massive receiving-box, to which are attached from two to half a dozen smaller hose with metal pipes, and nozzles attached, similar to those in use on fire-engines. The immense weight of water escaping through the pipes plays upon the bank of earth with great force, and, by playing upon the bottom and undermining, large caves occur by the action of the water, by which hundreds of tons of dirt are pulverized at once, and easily carried into the sluices by the water alone. There is often a larger quantity of water necessary, especially in soft ground, than can be forced through the pipes, and a stream is allowed to run over the bank and into the sluices.

By this means an enormous quantity of dirt can be washed daily, and even if the mine is comparatively poor, from the amount worked the pay is good, and in cases of rich diggings it is immense.

The gold thus washed out is saved by long strings or trains of sluices, of different widths and depths, according to the size of the mine and the quantity of water used. In the bottom of these sluices are placed "riffles," or false bottoms, of many

SLUICE MINING.

different kinds and shapes, according to the taste or judgment of those using them.

Perhaps as good a style as any in use is made from the blocks, three or four inches in thickness, sawed from the round bodies of trees. These blocks are secured in the bottom of the sluice, and from their shape, leave openings between them, in which the gold, from its weight, settles and remains,—the dirt and rocks going off with the water. At stated times the sluices are "cleared up;" that is, the blocks or "riffles" are removed, and the bottom of the sluice carefully washed and swept, the main part of the water having previously been turned off. In many localities quicksilver is used to collect and hold the fine gold.

At various times, in the early days of mining, gold was found in greater or less quantities in quartz, until the idea obtained that gold must be held only in the immense quartz ledges breaking out here and there over the face of the mountains.

Finally, some more adventurous than others turned their attention entirely towards these ledges, and but a short time had elapsed before the deep or underground system of mining was fairly inaugurated.

The "rastra" and mills took the place, in a great measure, of other methods of acquiring the precious metal. Some of the ledges were fabulously rich.

The Allison Ranch mine, as it was called, at one time was considered worth two millions of dollars. The Amador, in the county of the same name, paid its owner, Alvinza Haywood, one thousand dollars, net, per day. I only mention these as among the more prominent. But the whole State of California is filled with them, of greater or less value, and a century will see them still worked.

It was not until the year 1859 that silver attracted the attention of prospecters, and Nevada took a prominent place among the rich, mineral-producing countries.

This Territory, up to that time, was only known as the terror of immigrants,—with its deserts, and miles of barren, sage-covered plains and valleys.

Silver was first discovered in Nevada by a man named Comstock, in the year 1859, on Mount Davidson, in what is now known as the Comstock lode. The novelty of the discovery, and the inexperience of those who were interested in it, rendered it impossible, for a considerable time, to procure sufficient capital for the development of the new "find."

At last, the evident richness of the ore, and the fact that Mexico had an immense revenue from her silver-mines, caused capitalists and laborers to turn their steps towards the Washoe country, as it was all called in those days; and the silver interest grew until it fairly threw the search for gold in the shade for the time, and Nevada became the "Ophir" of the Pacific.

The Comstock lode was first struck on the side of Mount Davidson, above the present site of Virginia City, and nearly half a mile west of the present location of the works.

The cropping of the ledge and all the ore near the surface was very rich, and had to be hauled to Eagle and Washoe Valley for reduction, as the mills were located in those places. The method of reducing silver ore at that time was quite imperfect, and the "tailings," or residue, was often more valuable than the bullion extracted.

Upon sinking on the ledge in the different mines, which extends from north to south four or five miles, at a comparatively small depth, the ore-body gave out, and the opinion was freely expressed that the Washoe silver-mines had "gone up," to use the miners' vernacular.

But there was too much money already invested, and too many energetic men had interested themselves, to give up on so small a showing.

Then followed the dark days of the Comstock, while mines of every description, from Washington Territory to Arizona, were located and incorporated, and a perfect whirlwind of worthless "wild-cat" stock swept over the land. It was only necessary to show a piece of rock, accompanied by an assayer's certificate, and the stock would be freely taken by rich and poor. It was carried to such an extent that Mark Twain's story of a piece of grindstone giving an assay of several hundred dollars per ton was not much exaggerated. Every man had his pockets full of stock and his hands full of pieces of rock, until it seemed we were a race of geologists, and slightly mad at that.

As a matter of course the reaction must come, and it was terrible to legitimate mining interests. Still, through it all the *genuine* survived, and at last the Crown Point and Belcher mines struck a "Bonanza," and the future of Virginia and the Comstock was secured.

These two mines went up, and still up, in the market to fabulous figures, carrying with them all others in the vicinity, until locations which *never will* yield an ounce of bullion sold for hundreds of dollars per foot.

All things have an end, and so that deposit, though large, was finally worked out, and the Crown Point and Belcher pass away among the things that were, until further developments at a greater depth.

About the time of the temporary death of the two mines above mentioned the present "Bonanza," or ore deposit, was struck, completely eclipsing all former developments on the ledge, or in the United States, if not surpassing anything in the world yet discovered. The ore-body, first struck in the Consolidated Virginia, was found to extend into the California, and hopes were entertained that it also reached into the Ophir. But as yet there is no proof that such is the case.

The Comstock lode has been worked more or less for fourteen years. In that time it has yielded $150,000,000, or an average of $10,714,000 per year. The yield in 1859 was $14,000,000. It is probably more than that this year, and may be expected to average $15,000,000 for the next quarter of a century. No other lode has ever done so well. The Veta Grande, of Zacatecas, from 1548 to 1832, covering two hundred and eighty-four years, yielded $666,000,000, or $2,350,000 a year. The Potosi (Bolivia) mines, worked for over two hundred and fifty years, produced the enormous sum of $1,200,000,000, but that is less than $5,000,000 a year. It is said the Raymond and Ely yielded $4,000,000 in the year 1872. The silver-mines of Nevada and Utah, considering the short time they have been worked, are the richest in the world. The Consolidated Virginia has yielded from five to six hundred tons of ore per day for more than two years, and the California a like amount for several months.

What the future may bring forth time alone can tell, but with the experience of the past, and the energy and indomitable perseverance backed by enormous wealth of those engaged in prospecting, developments must continue to be made for ensuing ages.

During the years passed since the first discovery of silver, prospecting has been going on over the whole coast for silver, copper, and all other minerals and metals, with varied success. In the eastern part of Nevada large deposits of galena, or sulphuret of lead, have been found, all more or less argentiferous. In Eureka several large furnaces are in operation, with all modern improvements both for rapidity of working and facility for saving the precious metals. The bullion thus extracted is in bulk, mostly lead, but containing from two hundred to five hundred dollars per ton of gold and silver.

Other portions of the State are producing bullion of great amount, some fairly fine and some containing every possible variety of base metals, such as iron, zinc, antimony, nickel, etc. But the yield of silver in the aggregate is enormous, and the probabilities are in favor of an increase rather than diminution. But do not be alarmed, for silver will never remain a drug!

There have also been very large fields of borate of lime and soda found and worked, giving us as a home production borax, than which, perhaps, no more useful article could be found for the demands of our people.

We have also beds of sulphur, which are at

present being worked, and sulphuric acid manufactured with which is produced sulphate of copper, or the "blue-stone" of commerce, an article indispensable in amalgamating silver. Do not think we are a bad people because sulphur is so handy.

Coal is also found in several portions of the State, and in a few years undoubtedly we shall not need to import any fuel for our furnaces or chemicals for our mills. The whole country seems fitted to be self-sustaining in that which is and must be its support—its mines.

In no other portion of the habitable globe are fortunes made and lost so rapidly or with so little apparent effect. The millionaire of to-day and the pauper of to-morrow appears equally jolly, and the rush still goes on. But take it all in all it is far better for a man of small means to apply himself to a more safe and steady business. For mining speculations, like gambling, have a fascination from which it is very hard to break away.

So, my Eastern friends, do not commence. Keep out of the maelstrom, and your life will be happier and better in every respect. But if you *will* deal in stocks, do not, I beg of you, buy "wild-cats," or neglect to pay your assessments. It don't pay, and you will become a used-up "community" in a few months. Stick to dividend-paying mines, and never fail in collecting your dues as fast as declared, and you *may* be happy yet.

CHAPTER VI.

A GARDEN IN A GARDEN.

"Flowers look up to heaven, from whence
They have their nourishment,—
Moss-hid flowers, fragrant and concealed,
Like hidden charity."

ONE of the finest rides I ever had was down to San José (pronounced San Ho-za), by the bay fifty miles, and then by stage six. The sky is nearly always clear here in the summer-time. It was at that season of the year when I first visited this city. This made our journey exceedingly pleasant, as the air was warm, and we could see without limitation almost. The bay spread out around us like burnished silver, and the day was especially calm. The jewel of a little steamer that bore us down was not heavily burdened, so that our speed was not monotonous.

The scenery is delightful. Mountains lean against the sky, but far enough away to mellow the view. The valley was variegated with gathering harvest and ripening vegetation, for all grades are here to be seen, from planting the seed to the gathered sheaf.

Alviso was the landing-place of our steamer. This is some six miles from the bay, and is reached by the crookedest little creek, I suppose, a boat ever floated upon. The rank vegetation that lined its banks sometimes made it impossible to see it for more than fifty yards in advance of us.

I could not help but think, as I looked over the beautiful valley,—the Santa Clara,—of what Governor Hendricks, of Indiana, once said to me concerning this valley. "I do not think the garden of Eden ever equalled that valley," was his remark. I don't know about that. I have always had a good deal of profound veneration for that ancient garden, yet there were some opaque things about it; and there are some things about this valley that are objectionable, and why not? It is certainly earthly, but then it is very charming.

There are better agricultural districts in California, and with perhaps better climate; yet in many respects this is one of the most desirable spots in the State.

Our first impressions were of the best as we entered the town on the lovely street called Alameda. A grand Grange picnic was being held, which gave the general appearance of a gala day, and added to the attractions.

It is said this city has fifteen thousand inhabitants. Minus that number two thousand would perhaps be nearer the fact; but the difference, one way or the other, of a few thousand does not matter. You almost intuitively say, "How I should like to live here!"

I had letters of introduction to a friend in this city, which was quite an advantage to me in getting such information as I desired.

At this city was my first view of orange-trees, figs, etc., although they grow north of this, but I had not had an opportunity of seeing them. I was shown a field of barley that would yield a hundred bushels to the acre. The barley would average full five and a half feet in height. The owner said it was still growing at the rate of about an inch a day. It is marvellous what luxuriant growths are here seen in vegetation; and yet some other parts of the State excel this.

Real estate is high, and undoubtedly debars, somewhat, persons from locating here who otherwise like the place. The atmosphere is clear and pure, but in the evenings and mornings it is unpleasantly chilly to a new-comer, but, I suppose, very delightful to one used to it. They have frost occasionally, but never snow to as much as to cover the ground.

We would not detract an iota from the fair merits of Southern California, for that is the garden-spot of the State. But the whole State has been called a garden, and we certainly do no injustice in saying that this is a beautiful garden in a garden.

While it very materially differs from the southern part of the State, it has enough of the tropical in its character to make it delightful.

This is a section in which grow the most beautiful and fragrant flowers. And they sometimes present queer features. I saw three different colored roses, white, yellow, and red, all growing on one stalk. Here immense century-plants are sometimes seen growing in the streets. I could not but think of the labor and anxiety the ladies of the East have for their flowers, putting them in hot-houses, and by various means pressing and coaxing them to grow, and after all only partially succeed, while here some that are very rare in the East become a nuisance in their great growth.

In the East the ladies are delighted if they can make the English ivy grow a little in the house, where it is kept as a pet, while here it climbs over houses, fences and all, if they will but let it. And the scarlet geranium grows so luxuriantly that it is necessary sometimes to cut it down with an axe, like cutting saplings. And heliotropes grow to be large bushes.

This city has the distinction of being known as the Athens of California, as several fine institutions of learning are located here. A vast amount of local enterprise is manifested by San José and vicinity, more than in some Eastern cities of four times the inhabitants. A most beautiful boulevard has been built by the city to the distance of eight or ten miles, running east of the city to a noted summer resort. This makes one of the most delightful drives I have anywhere seen in the State. Some rows of eucalyptus-trees have been planted, and are growing very beautifully along the entire length of this boulevard, making, in addition to the drive, two delightful walks. Through the kindness of a friend I was driven the entire length of this road to Alum Rock, which seems to be quite a resort, as the boulevard is built to this point.

Alum Rock may, with some propriety, be called a mountain. This is literally saturated with alum. In some places you can gather clear, pure lumps as good as what you purchase from the apothecary. Just a little ways beyond is a clear, cold soda-spring, where we rested and slaked our thirst. Then close by is a bath-house for invalids, and not far off is another subterraneous tunnel bath arrangement,—I never learned what else to call it,—where gouty fellows bathe their painful limbs and backs. From under this flows an inky spring, whose waters are "black as night."

The city, I have learned, with its accustomed enterprise, proposes to erect commodious bath-houses here, and run them gratuitously, or for a very small fee. It is to be hoped it will be done, as it would undoubtedly be a great sanitarium for the afflicted.

The part of the valley through which the boulevard passes is as delightful a body of land, and forms as fine a view, as I ever saw. When this part of the State was being settled it was thought the land was of no account. Wild mustard, such as grows in the gardens in the East, literally covered the valley everywhere. It grew to the height of from ten to fifteen feet, and large enough for an ordinary-sized man to climb its stalks.

A prominent gentleman, one well known in California, whose word is perfectly reliable, told me himself that he many a time climbed the mustard-stalks, like climbing small saplings, to the distance of several feet from the ground just to test their strength. And he was a grown man. A ministerial friend told me that he knew of a Bible agent getting lost in this " grove of mustard," and did not find his way out for a number of hours.

The cattle that grazed upon the valley could not get through the thicket formed by the enormous growth, except where their travel would wear a path while the mustard was young. This shows the great richness of the soil. And the reader can well imagine the beauty of such a valley when the weeds and rubbish have been cleared away, and their places supplied by fruits and flowers of the richest and brightest kind. As far as eye can see is Nature's beauty charmingly displayed, brought out by the hands of toil and art.

Here are beautiful farms, winsome gardens, rich orchards with luscious fruit, tropical and semi-tropical productions, and large, comfortable residences.

San José has the distinction of being the Athens of California. It is not ours to dispute with her. She is linked on to Santa Clara, also a beautiful place, and the Alameda—the street that unites them—forms one of the finest drives in the entire country. Several institutions of learning are located here, the State Normal School and the University of the Pacific being the most prominent. The city has many very handsome residences and public buildings. Its churches and church influences are among the best west of the Rocky Mountains, being in an excellent condition, numerically and spiritually. This is a delightful place for a home, but openings for business are not very flattering.

CHAPTER VII.

NORTH OF THE BAY.

"The lesson which the many-colored skies,
The flowers, and leaves, and painted butterflies,
The deer's branched antlers, the gay bird that flings
The tropic sunshine from its golden wings,
The brightness of the human countenance,
Its play of smiles, the magic of a glance,
Forevermore repeat,
In varied tones and sweet,
That beauty, in and of itself, is good."—WHITTIER.

THE beauty of California must be seen in midwinter to be appreciated, and its distinct features and climatic effects are more plainly marked then than at any other time. Summer, so called, but in many places the real winter of the coast, is a time of parched ground, seared fields, and gathering harvests. It is much harder then to discern the essential difference of localities than in winter; you must form your opinion largely by that which chances to be seen, as matured products, for example. In winter, the humidity of the atmosphere is condensed into rain, so that one can tell the amount of the rain-fall in various localities,—a very important matter in California.

It had better be stated just here that the so-called "rainy season" of this State is a relative delusion to the Eastern man. It is a common thought in the East that "it never rains, but pours," in California during the wet season, so that it is a common expression, "I could not endure the *perpetual rain* for so many months."

Of course, there are freshets here occasionally, like in every other country where it rains. Some years ago the Sacramento Valley was inundated for miles upon miles on either side of the river. But that was a solitary instance in many years. Upon the contrary, the greatest want is more rain in the wet season.

At this very time, when the winter is very far advanced, stock are reported to be dying in great numbers in some sections in the southern half of the State from the want of water.

The rainy season in California, ordinarily, is about like a "wet April" in the Middle States. Copious showers mixed with sunshine, or whole days of rain, or whole days of clear, nice weather fill the time. But at no time is there that long, gloomy, cloudy, rainy, muddy, sickening weather so prevalent in the Eastern States. But where it rains, and where it rains enough, is by far a more important item than as to where it remains too much.

The effect and beauty of the winter are very

impressive, when going, as I did, direct from the snows and bleakness of the East down into the advanced spring-like appearance of the State.

I had never witnessed nor enjoyed so delightful a ride upon the bay as on this balmy February afternoon. In the summer-time the fierce winds make the water very rough, but now it was smooth and charming. The long line of thick, black smoke trailing from our steamer's chimney, and the foam in the track of the vessel, reflecting from its thousands of ripples the bright sunlight, while scores of gulls, white and plump as they are, sailed about us to gather the stray crumbs that fell upon the water, made a spectacle interesting to me. I could not help thinking of the poor lunatic's refrain,—

"I have ships that went to sea
More than fifty years ago;
None have yet returned to me,
But keep sailing to and fro.
I have seen them in my sleep
Plunging through the shoreless deep,
With tattered sails and battered hulls,
While *around them screamed the gulls*,
Flying low, flying low."

How strange to see at this time of the year such rank, tall weeds and grass! Yet such was almost the first thing we noticed on landing. We had not expected so much. Such shows the difference in the rain-fall north and south of the bay. Santa

Clara Valley, one of the finest in the State, lying south of San Francisco, is more apt to be affected by drouth than north of the bay. We were told that north of the bay they are never affected by drouth, but that sometimes, on the contrary, they have too much rain. To show the difference, it may be stated that now, in Santa Clara Valley, as rich as any part of the State, vegetation is only a few inches in height, while in Petaluma it is as many feet. The difference is owing to the rainfall. In many parts of the south, as already stated, the cattle are dying from the want of water, and in San Joaquin Valley the farmers, in many instances, have not sown their grain for the same reason; but here in Petaluma and Napa Valleys they have already had eighteen inches rain-fall this season.

By the kindness of a friend we were shown around the country, and through Sanoma County and over to Napa City.

Sanoma County, like its neighbor Marin, is devoted to the dairy business and fruit-raising. This is the great butter-making region of California, although the dairy business is quite largely carried on in many other sections.

An idea may be had of the magnitude of the butter business when it is known that one firm alone in Petaluma handles one million four hundred and sixty thousand pounds, or two tons per day. An average price paid to dairymen for butter is about thirty cents. This would make nearly half a million of dollars paid by this one firm for butter in a year.

Dairying is a very fine business. It does not necessarily involve much capital and requires little experience. The practice of renting dairies is very common. It is always done in the fall. In fact, all renting is done then. The usual terms in getting a dairy are to give half the receipts, or, if paid in coin, about twenty-five dollars per cow, and the owner furnishes everything, so that the renter has nothing to do but to move in and begin. Even the buckets, pans, and churns are all furnished ready for use. This includes, of course, the ranch or pasture-land.

It is counted that a cow will average one pound of butter per day,—sometimes more,—and safely calculated that she will be worth seventy-five dollars a year. Then there is the increase by calves that the renter gets. Hogs are always kept to use the surplus milk, and prove very profitable, because it costs virtually nothing to keep them.

A family with little means can secure ten or fifteen acres of land, keep a few cows and chickens, raise fruit, and make a fine living. An old Californian said to me, "We don't think that doing much. We will either make a good deal or break up." But if a man is satisfied to do so he can do well on but little capital.

Rev. Mr. Clifford kindly offered his services, horse and buggy, to show us the various features of this charming part of the country. This was far more pleasant than travelling by railroad, because we could take time to examine the country carefully. We objected decidedly to "Bill," the horse, although he was gentle enough, for he would not go under the American flag suspended over the street, and when we would sing he would attempt to run away. The religious character of the song made no difference whatever. I am confident that horse was opposed to the Electoral Commission and camp-meetings. But away from flags, and when we would smother our musical inclinations, he answered all our purposes, and helped us in gathering many an item.

Petaluma Valley is one large dairy on one side, and a gigantic vineyard on the other. Thousands of acres are devoted entirely to grape-culture, and immense wine-houses, in which are stowed great quantities of wine and brandy, are to be seen all along the mountains that hedge the valley. This is California's greatest curse. If the wine-making of the State could be stopped, the character of the people would be changed in a day. The variety and greatness of the productions of this State may prove its ruin yet.

This valley is very rich in soil, and sometimes land can be bought at a price bordering on reason. Good land ranges from one hundred to one hundred and fifty dollars per acre.

A chain of "young mountains or old hills" separates this from Sonoma Valley. But nearly all of these hills are subject to a high state of cultivation or to grazing.

Sonoma town, although an unimportant village now, once enjoyed the distinction for a brief space of time of being the State capital. That was in the time of "the Legislature-on-wheels," or rather when the State government was so restless that it remained only a short space of time at any one place.

The same high price of real estate is found here that is met everywhere in the State, although there is no outlet to this rich valley but by wagon-road. They have no railroad, and, what is very strange, they do not seem to want one. Napa City and Valley lie about twelve miles northeast of Sonoma. This valley, take it altogether, is the finest I have seen in the State; and aside from some topographical features, it is essentially different from the two valleys mentioned in this chapter. In Petaluma and Sonoma Valleys they cultivate very successfully potatoes and fruit. But I am informed that in Napa potatoes are not raised with much success, but that fruits are brought to a high degree of perfection. Potatoes are a staple article in California, but they cannot be cultivated in some places. So it is with nearly everything raised. It is necessary to determine what you desire to cultivate, and then select a place accordingly; that is, to buy your farm and then plant only what is adapted to the locality.

I was shown quite generally around the city and through the valley. The land is mainly devoted to farming. Large quantities of wheat are sown, and corn is raised with considerable success. Grapes, apricots, peaches, apples, pears, and almonds are cultivated very largely. The finest body of land I ever saw, I think, is in Napa Valley; it looks like one great garden. But high price is the bane. From Judge Hartson I learned a good deal in regard to the price and merit of real estate. The judge is enthusiastically in favor of Napa,—and that is right,—but we found him to be a very reliable gentleman.

Land immediately surrounding the city—say out as far as two miles—will run as high as four or five hundred dollars per acre. Some can be purchased at a less rate, but it is not the best.

The city is a very beautiful place, but not large, —not over five thousand inhabitants, and probably considerably less. The improvements are good and substantial. This is quite an educational centre. The city has good public schools; besides, there are

NAPA COLLEGIATE INSTITUTE.
(OF THE M. E. CHURCH.)

located here a Boys' School, under the influence of the Presbyterian Church, and a Young Ladies' Seminary—Miss McDonald, principal—under the patronage of the same denomination, and the Male and Female Collegiate Institute, under the control of the Methodist Episcopal Church. Professor L. L. Rogers is the president. This school is in a very fine condition, and exerts quite an extended influence, as do the others mentioned.

As an educational centre, Napa is very desirable as a place of residence. And its moral character is very good. It has substantial and well-attended churches, good schools, public spirit, kind people, a safe jail, and the largest insane asylum in the world, perhaps. But of course the two last-named public improvements are not designed for ordinary use.

I was told by the surgeon in charge that the asylum, counting for the various angles, is one mile in circumference. It is a grand building located in a grand country.

We made a visit to the celebrated natural soda springs, about six miles from the city. This is quite a novelty. Here about two hundred and fifty dozens of bottles are filled and shipped every day to all parts of the coast. The water is simply bottled as nature makes it, and is delightful to the taste. It is strongly impregnated with lime, magnesia, iron, etc.

It is no doubt a fine place to spend the hot season of the year, but we do not think it will ever pay for the capital that has and will be invested. Already two hundred and fifty thousand dollars have been spent on the springs, and it is proposed by the proprietor to erect a hotel the present season at an additional cost of a hundred thousand more. A stable is just being finished, all of stone, that has cost thirty-six thousand dollars. I have no doubt but these springs are valuable property, but I would much rather have the money that has been expended on them than to have the springs.

One of the finest places in the valley is Oak Knoll, the summer residence of Mr. Woodward, the proprietor of the celebrated gardens bearing his name. It is the source of great pleasure and profit, no doubt, to the owner, but, like thousands of similar places in California, it is a great detriment to the State. Here is a vast tract of land—twelve hundred acres, I understood—in the very heart of this fertile and charming valley, which is owned by one man, while there are thousands of families that are desirous of finding homes in this State. This entire valley is a rich farming country,—perhaps the best, take it all in all, in the State,—but it is monopolized by a comparatively few, or held at exorbitant prices. I would readily recommend this valley to persons coming to California, but the chances to buy property are not flattering.

North of Napa, towards Yountville and Calistogo, the scenery is finer and the land equally as rich, and prices not quite so high.

Market is quite convenient to all these points. The North Pacific Railroad runs right through the valley as far as Calistogo, and schooners come up as far as Napa. Freights are low, and a ready market is had at San Francisco.

I saw ripe, luscious apples by the bushel on the trees yet in this February day. But that is not surprising here. Some kinds would keep well on the trees until apples come again. There is no winter and but little frost to disturb them. In fact, here the flowers—certain species—bloom all winter in the open air. But this is a small matter, for they do the same as far north as the interior of Oregon.

This county—Napa—has not so many dairies as Sonoma, because there is far more agricultural land, I am informed. For the dairy business is confined more to the hills, which are suitable for grazing but not for farming. More can be made out of valley-land than turning it over to the dairy business.

One thing very greatly surprised me in these valleys and towns of which I have written in this chapter: that is, the amount of property for sale.

In town and country it is all the same. It is not possible that climate or health can enter into the matter, because the climate is delightful, and the health is as good as can be found in the State. One citizen said to me, "A Californian will sell his coat." I am inclined to think that is one reason,—every man will sell anything, if he gets his price. Then, I find there is a restless spirit, entirely inexplicable, among many of the people.

CHAPTER VIII.

A LAND OF MILK AND HONEY.

"As plays the sun upon the glassy streams;
Twinkling another counterfeited beam,
So seems this gorgeous beauty to mine eyes."
SHAKSPEARE.

THE old saying, that "one-half of the world don't know how the other half lives," is no more true than that the rest of the world knows but little of the merits and demerits of California in general, and Southern California in particular. "Distance lends enchantment" is as literally untrue in some things as it is true in others. It was somewhat true in the history of this State when gold was the all-absorbing item, and other commendable resources were not in the least developed. But now, since golden nuggets no more lie glittering on the plain as in the days of other years, distance really bedims the riches of this State. Although the gold-yield is greater than in California's palmiest days,—seventy millions were the product of the year 1876.

We say distance bedims the riches of this State, for is not California in a measure a world within itself? People here almost think so, and newcomers almost invariably feel so.

The prairies of the West are rapidly settling up with the sturdy immigrants from the East, thus extending the political and commercial powers of the American people; but the Rocky Mountains, the American Desert, and the Sierras are broad and barren enough to destroy, somewhat, the family domesticity. Salt Lake City only remains as the cartilage to hold together in feelings fraternal the Eastern Chang and Western Eng,—if the size of an intervening city has anything to do with fraternal relations.

It is, no doubt, a feeling of isolation that deters thousands of persons from coming to California,—persons who really ought to be here for pecuniary advantage or health.

Enterprise and means of enjoyment are here, but unlike those possessed in the East. But one line of railroad ties the desirable West to the lovable East, and that one seemingly very expensive in its fare, and, in some instances, domineering in its spirit.

In the East Cincinnati shakes hands socially with Philadelphia or New York, and they rub against Boston, Detroit, Chicago, and so on. But here San Francisco has not much of a neighbor in Sacramento, and Salt Lake is a thousand miles away; while San José, Santa Barbara, and Los Angeles are but youngsters growing up.

But what about the pros and cons of this part of the State,—the southern, absolutely, irrespective of neighborly kinsfolk? And the æsthetical and desirable features cannot be fully given in a single chapter. For reality outstrips even the imagination in this incomparable part of the world. Don't think we are infatuated with these beauties and resources beyond reason; not so, for we object to many things; but there is enough of the real, the true, and the beautiful to be admired by any one.

In some places, you know, human ingenuity and hard knocks have " made the wilderness to blossom as the rose." Not so here. The rose, the geranium, the daffodil, the heliotrope, and thousands of others of Nature's sweetest, brightest floral gifts, bloom all the year through, irrespective of man's lack or possession of horticultural knowledge, or the frigid prognostications of almanac-makers.

The interest of Southern California to the tourist is superior to that of the northern part of the State, while to the immigrant it is undoubtedly in advance, unless he desires to raise wheat or cultivate the apple-tree. And wheat will do just as well here as up north; but there is less agricultural land, hence this staple product would of necessity be curtailed. Apples want a sharper distinction of seasons than can be found here. For them there must be a time for "winter's embrace" as well as "summer's fruitage." A distinction of seasons seems to add to the flavor of this fruit. But apples are raised in Southern California with very fine success.

No doubt some of the difference between the northern and southern parts of the State depends upon the taste of the person.

North they have higher mountains, broader plains, bigger farms, more rivers, larger cities, and perhaps as rich a soil, while in the south there are better climate, richer fruits of tropical growth, in greater abundance to the area of country, larger vegetable productions, and less chilly weather and less heat in summer.

Here winter(?) comes in midsummer, and no snow whatever falls. Outside of mountain districts snow is an entire stranger.

The valleys of the south, clear to Lower California, are in general of the richest quality of soil, and adapted to the growth of nine-tenths of the productions of the tropical and semi-tropical regions.

In many places irrigation is a necessity, but along the coast it is often not absolutely essential, as the fogs from the sea during the night furnish a sufficient amount of moisture.

In the vicinity of Santa Barbara I saw vegetation growing very finely in July and August, with no artificial irrigation. Corn was doing well, although no rain had fallen for more than three months.

Santa Barbara is one of the most lovely places in Southern California. The climate, soil, temperature, all are very delightful. The summer temperature of this city is that of Boston, while the winter is precisely that of Norfolk, Virginia. It is situated in the isothermal lines of these two localities. The mean temperature is a little above 60°. In the summer-time no fires are necessary at all, while in December and January but a slight amount is required.

The evenness of the temperature, the purity of the atmosphere, and the want of the high winds that are more prevalent in northern and higher sections of the State, make this place quite a sanitarium for the sick. The impression that this is a very unhealthy locality is sometimes made upon persons here, until they have learned that these ghostly-looking and coughing persons have sought this city as a refuge from immediate death. My opinion is, that, notwithstanding the healthful advantages of Santa Barbara, there are many places in Southern California with *natural* advantages fully equal to this in point of health.

The soil in this locality is very rich. However, the agricultural land is not very extensive. The valley in which the city is located is narrow, being perhaps not more than three miles in width at this point. The topography of the country and the character of the soil are especially favorable to horticulture. Be it said just here, that there are two reasons for the great and rapid growth of vegetation in this country. First, the soil is rich, and adapted to agricultural and horticultural products. Then the temperature and atmospheric conditions are such that vegetation grows *all the time*. The heat of the day does not urge a growth that will be retarded by the chilly night, as in the East.

I saw the blue gum-tree (*Eucalyptus globulus*) twelve inches in diameter and *thirty feet in height* at the age of two years. I saw in a gentleman's yard near the city sprouts of the same species six feet high as the growth of four months. In the orchard of the same gentleman I counted *one hundred and fifty* peaches, plump and nice, on a tree no higher than my cane,—three feet. The geranium grows, hither and yon, like great clumps of bushes, which they are. The flat-leaved cactus (*Opuntia*), that I have seen in the East, after much coaxing, grow to the height of a foot or so, here is to be seen as high as a house, while the club cactus (*Opuntia Bylovii*) grows even taller. I have seen the elder, the same kind I used to gather in the East with such zest in my boyhood days, to manufacture into spiles, used in tapping trees, at sugar-making, having the thickness of twelve inches, perhaps more; while it is necessary sometimes to climb the castor-bean-tree with the assistance of a ladder to gather the fruit. Here was my first sight of the pepper-tree (*Schinus molle*). It is peculiarly beautiful in its fine pinnate foliage drooping gracefully, like the weeping-willow, and hung with racemes of large, red, currant-like fruit. It ornaments a city beautifully, and it is said the aroma given off is very healthful. Here figs grow very luxuriantly, and are very productive. This is one of the most beautiful trees I ever saw. It never blossoms, but puts out its fruit without any bloom,—the sign

"That summer dawns o'er all the land."

I was told that one peculiarity of the fig-tree is that the more the fruit is plucked the more it bears,—quite suggestive to many people. I have seen fig-bushes not half a yard in height loaded with this delightful fruit.

This city enjoys the ordinary distinction of having its streets "run at right angles," but they do not point directly to the cardinal points of the compass. I never could get reconciled, while there, to the positions of east, west, north, and south.

As has already been intimated, this is held, especially by the inhabitants of the town, as the greatest health resort in America. We have no reason to question its health-giving qualities,—for they are very fine,—but there are other localities that are just as good sanitariums. Santa Barbara, as an English town, is less than ten years old, although as a Spanish settlement its age laps even centuries. A century after Columbus discovered America, when Cabrillo sailed up the coast he found quite a population here, and spent several months among them.

But notwithstanding a resident Spanish population of more than three hundred years, the resources of the country and quality of the soil were never tested till Anglo-Saxon vim and skill took possession. Even yet the country is not more than half yielding its store of products. I was greatly surprised when I first went to Santa Barbara to find that most of the fruit and vegetables used by the city were being shipped from San

Francisco. This was strange, when vegetables grow most luxuriantly in the soil here. Water is not scarce. The Mission Water Company seems to have an inexhaustible supply; besides, this is one of the points where irrigation is not so great an essential as in some other localities.

As far as physical labor is concerned, here is one of the easiest places in the world to live.

The old Spanish Mission stands about two miles from the wharf, and has a most delightful view of the bay and the islands beyond. This old church is of Moorish architecture, and dates its beginning back more than a hundred years.

Nearly everything is built of stone cemented with a very durable kind of cement; hence there is very little labor necessary to keep up repairs.

A lazy, careless life is that of those monks whose home is in this venerable retreat. As I wandered through the spacious halls and into the chapel,—ornamented with scenes in fresco of the Passion and crucifixion of our Lord, and the various representations of the cross,—and heard echoing over the galleries, from some invisible point, the tremulous strains of the organ played in some minor key; when I saw the æsthetical features of the Romish religion prominently displayed; the sombre sanctity that pervaded every department; I could partially understand the great power that Church has over certain minds.

In addition to the healthful advantages of this city, there are springs with strong medicinal qualities located some four miles from the town. They are situated about a thousand feet above the level of the sea, and are said to be very beneficial to persons suffering with gout or rheumatism. I tried a bath and found it very refreshing; but more thrilling, by far, was the view I had of the ocean from this elevated point, in the clear sunlight and pure air of this delightful locality.

This city has very fine advantages. Hotels among the best outside of San Francisco are here. But we must confess, as we are writing for the benefit of the public and not for private individuals, that the charges are entirely too high. In some instances it amounts to downright "fleecing." Hundreds of people, mostly of the sickly sort, visit this city in the course of the year, and it should be remembered that many invalids who need the climate of Santa Barbara belong to the poorer class. One lady here said to the writer, "We *expect* to live off of the people that come here." And so we thought.

This county is fully a hundred miles in length, running northward beyond Point Conception, and is adapted to almost all the fruits except oranges, and these do fairly well if sheltered from the winds.

During my sojourn at this city I was, by the kindness of a friend, invited to accompany him to the beautiful town of San Buenaventura, and the Santa Clara and Ojai Valleys. This was one of the most pleasing and profitable trips I ever took in the Golden State. My friend, Rev. John R. Tansey, with whom I enjoyed these few days of recreation and observation, was one of the most genial of men. He had a spirit as musical and as mellow as is ever the lot of mortals to possess. He has since died, leaving behind him the benediction of a symmetrical character and an exemplary life.

Our journey lay through the delightful country surrounding the neighborhood of Carpenteria,— a section where tropical and semi-tropical fruits blushed and looked enticing on either side of the road, while graceful palms nodded to us as we passed. Gathering harvests of wheat and barley, and tall, rank corn were the connecting links between the temperate zone and the tropical appearance. Immense trees of the live-oak species furnished numerous shades along the way, while the scenery on our left was made grand by the bold, rugged spurs of the Santa Inez Mountains, sometimes lying off in the distance, then pressing so near the ocean that lay on our immediate right as to drive us into its breakers, where our faces were dampened by the spray. It is said, "time and tide wait for no man;" and thus we found it, for the tide allowed us to pass these sea-washed points only at certain intervals. This charming part of Southern California is not the best place for the poor man, for, as we have said before in this chapter, the valley is narrow and pretty well filled, and property is held at a high price.

San Buenaventura is situated at the lower end of the Santa Clara Valley,—one of the richest in the southern part of the State. North of this some twelve or fifteen miles is the Ojai (pronounced O-hi), a rich, fertile section, finely sheltered by the mountains that surround it. Here in these valleys land can occasionally be purchased at quite reasonable rates, unless it be that which has been cultivated and improved. The latter kind brings a high price generally. For the country is healthy, the land very productive, and the people prosperous; hence there are few that want to sell. In this county farms can be had as rich as any that are under cultivation, that only want the plough and a few years' labor to make them equal to these desirable homes that dot here and there the valley. The town is rapidly settling up with a kind, industrious class of people, many of them from the Middle States. The main products of this county are fruit, wheat, and wool, of which large quantities are shipped from this port.

CHAPTER IX.

A LAND OF MILK AND HONEY.—*Continued.*

> "No tongue—all eyes; be silent."—TEMPEST.
>
> "Men's eyes were made to look; and let them gaze."
> ROMEO AND JULIET.

AN unimportant telegram from my friend, whose kindness gave me the information contained in the last chapter, was the cause of my seeing the cities and places of so much interest in the most southerly part of the State.

The overland route by stage is one of great interest, but it is very fatiguing,—stage-riding always is. The distance from Santa Barbara to Los Angeles is about a hundred miles, and from the latter city to San Diego fully a hundred and fifty miles. By the steamer down the coast is the pleasantest, if one is not compelled to pay tribute to the realm of Neptune,—

> "The watery kingdom, whose ambitious head
> Spits in the face of heaven."

But there are few persons so constituted as not to be troubled by sea-sickness. I never could help becoming sick, even as the steamer babbles at the wharf. But the steamer-ride from Santa Barbara to San Pedro, the point for disembarking for Los Angeles, is one of the finest down the entire coast, for the cluster of islands out of Santa Barbara Bay, and occasionally down the coast towards San Diego, seem to shelter the steamers from rough seas. From San Pedro to Los Angeles is about thirty miles,—as rich a stretch of country as ever was kissed by a sunbeam, and yet it was long thought to be worthless, although the wild weeds grew from ten to fifteen feet in height.

They now have many very fine artesian wells in this county and along the line of railroad from San Pedro to Los Angeles. These wells are from one hundred to one hundred and fifty feet in depth. In one or two instances they were compelled to sink near three hundred feet. These are of inestimable value to the landholder, as they furnish water needed for irrigation that could not be found anywhere else. There are very few fences on the ranches, which gives a bare look to the farms. And in the dry, parched condition of summer, the general appearance of the country where there are no artesian wells or irrigation is not very cheery.

The olive-orchards, the English walnuts, the almond-groves, and lemon- and orange-trees, as you near the city, are extremely beautiful, covered with blossoms, or golden fruit, luscious and tempting,—

> "'Twere worth ten years of peaceful life,
> One glance at their array."

My first view of Los Angeles and vicinity was in August, and hence an unfavorable time. The valleys looked parched and dry, save here and there where the artesian wells poured out their waters, causing vegetation to look fresh and green, like so many oases in a desert. These artesian wells may be said to be an inestimable advantage to this country, yet there is no doubt but there are disadvantages connected with them. For there are, unquestionably, malarious influences attending them. The rank vegetable growths produced by these wells of water must, as a matter of course, sooner or later decay, which will tend to produce sickness.

My lamented friend, referred to before in this chapter, was grandly situated on a very fine ranch in the vicinity of Florence, upon which were two overflowing wells. The immediate benefit of artesian wells was manifest in the vegetable growths along the streams of water running from them.

Los Angeles County, like all parts of California, and the southern part especially, bears very plainly yet the evidences of old Spanish rule and customs. The old Mission still stands, and many of the adobe houses,—houses that are made of unpressed sun-dried bricks. They have the most primitive look, but are very comfortable and quite durable. The old Franciscan monks still carry on a lazy kind of something called a religious school, but they are of such a dreamy kind of character that it is a misnomer to call them anything that means benefit or industry.

The town (Pueblo) of Nuestra Senora de Los Angeles, " under and in conformity to an order of the then Governor of California, Phelipe de Neve, dated at the Mission of San Gabriel, August 26, 1781, was founded in a formal manner on the 4th of September of the same year."

The founders of the town numbered twelve adult males, all heads of families. We would here give their names, but it would be folly, because it might produce serious results, for, like half the names in California which are of Spanish-Mexican origin, no novice in the world can pronounce them without danger to his vocal organs. These founders had been soldiers at the Mission of San Gabriel, and although discharged from Spanish service continued to draw rations and salary, because they founded this "City of the Angels," we suppose. Grand old days, when men were supported at public expense because they started a town! Could we but have the same custom again, how many towns we would have! City of the Angels! What's in a name? Nothing, you would readily think, if you could from to-day look back through its history of nearly a hundred years. These old monks, in their line, evidently thought there was much power in names, for they have exhausted the whole catalogue of saints and then make irreverent combinations, such as *Jesus Maria*, and so on, to furnish names for their *pueblos*. If they could have only breathed the sanctity of the persons who first had these names upon these towns, it would have been a great assistance to the missionary of to-day. This town is no mean place, yet its present history, and certainly its past, would not indicate that it would be taken as the abode of angels.

The total number of souls comprising the first settlement of this city was forty-six. Twenty of these were children under ten years. Of the twelve founders, two were natives of Spain, one a native of China, and the other nine from the following places: Sinaloa, Sonora, and Lower California.

In early days the government of California was a queer admixture of military and ecclesiastical powers, so it can be readily inferred that the municipal government of Los Angeles was a compound of political and military, and the predominancy in favor of the latter. The absence of municipal records for the first half-century of the founding of Los Angeles is, at least, presumptive evidence that the municipal officers exercised but little authority in that period of its history.

The growth of the real city of Los Angeles— that is, since the Americans came with their energy and capital—has been very rapid but substantial. It is scarcely twelve years since it began to be developed as an American town, and yet there is hardly a city in the entire country that excels it in beauty and substantial improvements. It does not depend upon mining excitements, nor the imaginary advantages that are so often advertised to "draw" the people. But it is backed up by the finest agricultural lands in the entire State.

Los Angeles' permanency is assured in the durability of the climate, and rich country surrounding it. But its magnitude as a city of large dimensions depends upon two or three as yet uncertain matters. If the Southern Pacific Railroad should ever be built, this city would of necessity be greatly benefited by it, whether it should be the terminus or not. Then it has for a number of years been thought by many that California would be divided into two States. If this should occur, which it will sooner or later, Los Angeles would be the southern capital. Quite recently has the theory been advanced of setting off Southern California by running a line due east from Point Conception, and then taking a slice from Arizona and giving it to the part set off, and thus form a new State. This would make a very respectable State in size, being fifteen or twenty times larger than some of the Eastern States, but it would be "rough on Arizona." If this should be done, as it may, it would make Los Angeles the "eye of the State." And we are half inclined to think she has "an eye on" such a change.

In 1866 the total assessed valuation of property in the county was a little more than $2,000,000. Now, just a decade, it is $15,000,000. The entire population of the county in the year given was 10,000. Now it is more than 30,000. Then the city had about 5000. Now it has 13,000. The county is rapidly filling up with a class of immigrants that are superior in social, intellectual, and religious endowments. These give Los Angeles City and County a character that shines very brightly alongside of some localities in the State where they profess a high standard of morality. The Sunday-law is closely observed, and the Sabbath is held to be a day of rest and religious enjoyment. The morals of the place are as good as can be found in the State. The desirableness of Los Angeles as a place of residence is manifest somewhat in the rapid growth of the city, already alluded to. The heat is a little intenser in the summer than at Santa Barbara or San Diego, but milder in the winter, not having so much dampness from sea-breezes. To the new-comer the heat of summer seems quite severe at first, but one soon becomes used to it; besides, it is always moderated by slight winds in the middle of the day.

At Fort Yuma, in the southeastern part of San

Diego County, the mercury will indicate in the summer-time 120° in the shade, while in Arizona it will even go higher. At Los Angeles the mean temperature of January is about 47°; of February 51°; of March, 53°; of April, 64°; of May, 68°; of June, 73°; of July, 75°; of August, 77°; of September, 72°; of October, 69°; of November, 61°; of December, 57°. These calculations are made from the meteorological table kept of the year 1876, and of course will be considered a fair average.

The table was made from four observations daily,—7 o'clock and 10 o'clock A.M., and 3 o'clock and 6 o'clock P.M. The coldest hour marked that year was on the 23d of December, at 7 A.M., when the mercury fell to 41° above zero. The highest temperature indicated in the whole year was 93°, which was at 3 P.M. of August 1 and 2. The greatest variation of monthly temperature was in May, when a range of 38° was indicated by the thermometer. The average temperature of Los Angeles City for the year 1876 was 65°.

These are actual figures of the temperature of last year, and may be relied on. It is often said that this city is so hot in the summer as to be almost unendurable. The reader will see that the figures do not so indicate it. Our imaginary feelings sometimes overleap the boundary of facts, and even deceive us. To one going to Los Angeles in midsummer it seems very, very hot, because his feelings are touched by the parched condition of things caused by the long dry weather, whereas the temperature may be lower than at his Eastern home.

Los Angeles furnishes desirable places for homes; the temperature need not debar any one. Two objections do arise, however, that must not be overlooked in this chapter. The same mistake is made here that is made in many other places of the State, in having the prices of real estate too high. To pay from fifty to two hundred dollars for unimproved and uncultivated farm-land is simply to give more than it is worth. Southern California is meritorious, but there is a point beyond which prices may be unreasonable, notwithstanding merit. Then there is a strong probability of droughts every few years. To be sure, they are never ruinous, but they are a great disadvantage. Many of the productions of Southern California are either of such a nature, or mature at such a time, as not to be affected by the dry weather. The tropical and semi-tropical fruits are raised here in great abundance; oranges, on account of the steady, warm temperature, are among the very reliable productions of Los Angeles County. A full-grown orange-tree is expected to yield from forty to sixty dollars' worth of fruit every year, and sometimes even higher. And it seems that age but adds to their capacity for bearing. It takes ten years, from planting the seed, for the orchard to begin to pay, hence it is not a very speedy way to get an income from money invested.

The silk-culture is just now beginning to attract a good deal of attention in this county. The natural facilities for such an enterprise are unquestionably good, judging from the characteristics of the countries where the silk-worm is produced.

The best place to purchase property sometimes is in one of the colonies that are located in the county; this is not always the case, however. These colonies are companies of men that have bought large tracts of land and laid them out in various-sized lots, as small farms. The companies usually have water facilities provided, besides trees and shrubbery set out, and sometimes small orchards planted, so that a home is well started when the purchase is made. This is very desirable if too great a price is not offered for present improvements. Water is the main item in California, and it is always the best to own your own water, then you are independent.

There are ninety thousand acres under cultivation this year in Los Angeles County. This makes ten thousand more than any previous year.

The proportions are about as follows: barley twenty thousand, corn twenty thousand, wheat ten thousand, hay five thousand, potatoes two thou sand, rye twelve hundred, oats eight hundred, and fruit and miscellaneous products take up the rest.

Riverside is one of those enterprising villages that have, like the marvellous vegetable growths of this country, sprung up as by magic. Nor is it like many of the mountain towns, a "hot-house affair," whose development and existence depend upon imaginary valuations or spasmodic productions. Towns grow very rapidly on this coast, and, anon, decline just as suddenly. Houses have been built for fifty thousand dollars and upwards, in which hundreds of thousands of dollars' worth of business have been carried on in a twelvemonth, that to-day stand perfect and good, with not an occupant but the owls and bats. And these same houses need not even be "bought for a song," for occupancy will give undisputed possession. The same holds good in reference to once large towns. Columbus, in Esmeralda County, Nevada, a half-dozen years ago, had a population of ten or twelve thousand, and fine residences valued at thousands of dollars, whereas, less than a year ago, it had fewer than a hundred inhabitants. Como (classic name), in Lyon County, of the same State, was once a thriving village of several hundred people; but to-day it enjoys the poetry of silence, save the noise of the wind and wild beast as they go through the streets, for not a solitary inhabitant is there. These are but illustrations of many other places in like condition. I have seen fine residences on once popular thoroughfares, built by immense outlays of money, that are to-day without an occupant, and not even sold for taxes, as no one appears to buy.

Of course, these are in localities that once were supported by the mines, and had no other resource to depend upon. Hence, when the mines failed, property was bound to go down.

Not so regarding the substantial parts of California. No country in the known world is more productive than the agricultural lands of the Pacific Coast. Not even the lands of Bashan and Palestine excelled this. And many characteristics of the two countries are quite similar.

These agricultural lands will last forever, and many of them grow better every year as the soil is tilled. Town and city property may and will fluctuate in valuation, as local and national matters affecting commerce come to the surface and then recede again. But as desirable, valuable property, these sections that are not dependent upon the mere *ipse dixit* of stock-brokers, or the imaginary wealth of a mine, will never become worthless, but continue to grow in valuation. They are more valuable than bank accounts, as bank accounts sometimes are on this coast, because California lands are never "unfortunate" enough to "fail."

Five years ago, where the town of Riverside

now stands, was a sun-scorched desert, used for nothing but a sheep-range, where the herds were driven to graze. Now it is a settlement of twelve hundred inhabitants, with all the delights that a semi-tropical country can give. This town is an evidence of the energy and enterprise of this advanced age. Many places in Southern California and in this county are evidences of great success, but none, take it all together, has excelled this. We cannot say, for it is not true, that Riverside surpasses other localities, but in climate, soil, and location it certainly is very desirable.

It is situated in a magnificent plain, surrounded by a most picturesque mountain range.

The Santa Ana River runs at its feet, and the beautifully wooded country of the Jurupa (Hooroopa) stretches away in front.

"Standing in the centre of the plain, a poetical panorama of unrivalled beauty delights the observer. There is Riverside in the centre, its handsome white houses nestled among the evergreen foliage. In every direction blooming orange-groves look resplendent, as the ardent beams of the southern sun dance among the branches. Delightful lawns, shaded by the majestic eucalyptus, the tapering fir, the blooming magnolia, and the graceful pepper-tree, stretch out in all points around the town. Pellucid streamlets meander lazily along through the streets. Ornamental trees of really tropical luxuriance bloom out in every possible nook. A delicious perfume suggests the presence of flower-beds, and the suggestion is correct. Interspersed among the orange-groves are verdant patches of alfalfa meadow, giving a charming effect to the outline of the landscape. For miles across the plains coquettish-looking white cottages peep out from their surrounding shades of foliage.

"The landscape, in its evergreen luxuriance of growth and richness of color, is strikingly tropical in feature. So rapid has been the growth of the trees, so enormous is the wealth of vegetation, that Riverside already looks like a settlement of thirty years' growth.

"With the purple light of the setting sun streaming in broken beams on the orange- and eucalyptus-groves, and through the cypress-, fir-, and pepper-trees; the majestic crest of Grayback and the undulating slopes of Mount San Jacinto growing fiery red in the distance; Mount San Antonio and the San Gabriel range half hidden by a dazzling golden lustre; the crests of the Temescal just visible through a fiery haze; the southern hills looking weird and shadowy in the receding light; the Santa Ana just visible through the verdant woods of the Jurupa; and the emerald valley of San Bernardino bright to the north, Riverside is one of the most beautiful of landscapes."

Riverside is a combination of three old colonies,—the Southern Californian, the New England, and the Santa Ana,—and contains now about ninety square miles, being about eighteen miles in length by five in width,—an area as large as some of the principalities of the Old World.

The want of water is met here by two canals, built for irrigating purposes, which furnish a supply commensurate with present or any demand that is likely to be made in the near future. The present capacity of the canals is nine thousand miner's inches. Surface water is found at no great depth, and artesian wells can be sunk without much trouble or expense.

In our opinion land is held at too high a price at present. It ranges from twenty-five to fifty dollars per acre. No sales are made except to actual settlers. Thus every land-owner at once improves his own farm, and does not, in letting it lie, become wealthy by the labor of other men without helping in turn to advance the property of the entire community. There is undoubtedly a disposition, in California in general, and Southern California in particular, to give a florid coloring to all prospects and openings. To be sure, there is a great deal to "puff," for Nature has done a wondrous amount for this country. And no objection would be made to all the advertising that might be done if, when the charming features of the country are published, prices were always reasonable, and not co-extensive with the amount of praise given. By this remark it must not be thought that we underestimate these great advantages and Nature's blessings. We do not, and we have no fear that the average reader will think so when he has read these pages. But it is true that the prices of real estate and so forth are often based upon the willingness of Nature to bless these rich plains, and not upon the absolute value of the property. For instances, there are many places here that have unexceptionable climate where property is held at exorbitant prices. To be sure, the probabilities of agricultural or vegetable productions are equivalent to climatic benefits, but valuations are based largely on climate, as though God intended that pure air should be subject to the laws of barter. If an analysis could be made of a property valued at, say $500, it would stand something like this: Land and improvements, 20 acres, $300; clear sky, $50; climate, $100; and fine perspective, $50; total, $500. Many a square yard of climate has been sold at a good round price that was never reckoned in the sale.

And nobody denies that these articles should be considered somewhat in the sale, but the objection is that so much valuation should be placed upon these advantages at once, as though they were late productions, and not as old as time.

Riverside is not an exception to this fact. It is a splendid locality, and is settling up with immigrants from the East, just as all Southern California is doing, but it is so because disease and horrible climate are driving them here, and not because extraordinary low prices allure. But for this reason this would be a good place for the poor man. Everything can be produced here that grows in semi-tropical countries.

Eight crops of alfalfa are gathered here annually. As much as eighteen tons of this hay is harvested from an acre. Some of the citizens fatten hogs on this grass. A ten months' hog was killed here a while ago that netted four hundred and twenty-five pounds, and was fed on alfalfa alone till two weeks before being slaughtered. The fig is raised here with very fine success, and the orange is already very extensively cultivated. Over sixty thousand of these trees are planted, and during the season forty thousand more will be under cultivation. The lemon, lime, English walnut, citron, and pomegranate are being very extensively planted. But none of these, unless it is the walnut, will equal in profit the orange. An acre of aged orange-trees will yield from twelve to eighteen hundred dollars.

This colony produced during the year 1876 six hundred and fifty thousand pounds of white Muscat raisins, which are considered equal to any that are imported.

Aside from Riverside, there are Colton, a town less than a year old, and old San Bernardino, not to speak of a number of other very desirable localities, all possessing the usual advantages already spoken of, except the one great necessary article,—water. And in many sections this is being provided for by water canals or artesian wells. As already stated in this chapter, these wells can be sunk at a comparatively little cost, and almost anywhere in the valleys. But as long as the country can dispense with them it should do so, for they undoubtedly will engender malarias, and produce unhealthy changes in the country. Of course, in some sections artesian wells are a necessity, for they are the only source of water, and without it these sections are an arid waste. Much valuable land can now be bought in comparatively remote places at a low price, that only requires the use of a little capital in sinking artesian wells to make it as valuable as any now under cultivation.

This is a land of gigantic distances, which, anon, do not lend the "enchantment" of which the poet wrote. And then again they do; for the farther one gets away from some localities we wot of, after the first view, the more enchanting they appear. This facetious sentence must not be given any force, save to a portion of this country. A part of it is a vast waste or desert that never can be worth a penny.

This is perhaps equal to an area of eight thousand square miles.

As these figures are given of the desert part, let not the reader suppose that none is left that is arable or valuable. Does it not seem decidedly newsy that San Bernardino County itself, but a small part of the great State of California, is larger than either Connecticut, Delaware, Maryland, Massachusetts, New Hampshire, New Jersey, Rhode Island, Vermont, West Virginia, to say nothing of the District of Columbia? Though only a county, it shows comparison with its fellows, the counties of its own or any other State, and even leaves behind the respectable areas of nine States. It equals the aggregate area of Connecticut, Delaware, Massachusetts, Rhode Island, and New Jersey. It is nearly as large again as Maryland; more than twice as large as Vermont; nearly three times as large as New Jersey, and almost five times as large as Connecticut; eighteen times as large as Rhode Island, and three hundred and eighty-four times the size of the District of Columbia.

San Bernardino County is more than ten times larger than eight of the dynasties of Europe and the Feejee Islands combined, and more than one-third larger than Switzerland.

There is land enough capable of immediate cultivation to give eighty thousand families a farm of eighty acres to the family, or to one hundred and sixty thousand families forty acres to the family, —a very respectable amount in this productive country; and counting five to the family, nearly a million of persons can live comfortably on the land subject to cultivation in this great county. And besides this there are tens of thousands of acres, as rich in soil as any now under cultivation, that only require irrigation to make them as desirable as any now being tilled. Abundance of water is to be had for irrigation for all the lands that are likely to be taken up for some time to come. Some times it is held at a high price, but the water is there.

This county has the best openings for immigrants of any part of the State, all things considered. To be sure, so large an area as this county has must have a great variation in topography, and even in climate. It is in these respects a county of contrasts. The southern slope is semi-tropical in climate and productions, while the northern and eastern parts are merely a volcanic waste, useless for either agriculture or grazing. This mountainous desert, however, is very rich in all kinds of metals. These mineral deposits have hitherto been but little developed, because of the want of means of transportation. The completion of the Southern Pacific Railroad now furnishes excellent facilities for transporting the products of these mines to good markets, so it may be expected that mining in this county will soon become very active.

The resources of San Bernardino are mineral, agricultural, and pastoral. The agricultural productions range from the vegetable of the frigid zone to the limes of the tropics. The chief agricultural productions are wheat, barley, oats, rye, corn, beans, peas, peanuts, castor-beans, and beets.

Nowhere in the world, as we have already intimated in another chapter, does the beet grow to so great a size as in California, and nowhere in the State does it attain to a greater size than in this county. If works for the manufacture of beet-sugar were erected here or in Los Angeles County, beet-culture would become one of the most profitable industries of the entire valley.

The California beet is in every way superior to the French beet. The former has eight per cent. of sugar, while the latter has but six. In this county there is little or no frost whatever, hence this vegetable is allowed to remain in the ground during the entire winter, thus saving all the saccharine matter. Whereas if the beet had to be gathered to avoid the frost and stowed away, much of the sugar would be lost.

This is absolutely a fruit county. The apple of the north grows well by the side of the orange and the lemon. Yet, for flavor, the apple requires a keener distinction of the seasons than is found here. There is no doubt whatever but apples have a much better flavor where there are sharp winters than where the climate is even all the year round. But the orange and lime, the fig, pomegranate, the grape, and all semi-tropical fruits attain here to perfection. Here the stately palm seems to be in its native element.

The vegetables adapted to both the temperate and semi-tropical countries are raised here to perfection. The Irish potato grows with fine success in the elevated mountain valleys, while the sweet potato flourishes in low, sandy soils. Cabbages, turnips, squashes, pumpkins, and melons attain to their greatest growth in San Bernardino County. It is almost incredible how quickly the latter vegetable will mature from the time the seed is put in the ground. Melons have ripened in three weeks from the time the seed was planted.

Owing to the isolation of this county before the railroad was completed, which made it relatively inaccessible, good land has been cheaper here than in any other part of the State. But as settlers came in the price of land has been inflated. At present, for naturally damp land, or land with good irrigating facilities, prices range from fifty to one hundred dollars per acre, according to location. Whether for agriculture or pomology, there is doubtless no better land in the State.

This county is famous for its dried grapes, which

bring the best price in all the markets, while its raisins are said to excel those of any other part of the State; but perhaps this is putting it quite strong.

There is yet much valuable land open to preemption, but the most of it is still unsurveyed. In fact, only a few townships are established, and they lie near the towns.

It is a mistake and a disadvantage to the county that these fine arable lands are yet unsurveyed, for if they were there would be a more rapid influx of immigration. Men do not want to settle upon land of whose boundaries they can possibly have no knowledge. One great disadvantage of this, as well as most of the counties of California, is in the want of perfect titles. There are good titles, that have been sifted thoroughly, but to know just which they are is difficult to ascertain without a good deal of care. No warranty deeds are given; the purchaser must be content with a "quit claim." I have no doubt but this is one of the greatest barriers to a rapid settling up of this country.

Expenses in all Southern California are of necessity much lighter than in the East. Improvements are not so extensive. A dwelling-house can be built for little more than half the money it would cost in the East. One of the chief cares in building is rather to prevent the effect of the heat than to debar the cold. The mean summer temperature is not far from 100°, and the winter in the neighborhood of 60°,—giving an average mean of 80°. Thus it will be seen that the influence of the cold is not burdensome. These figures are not from any official statement, but nearly approximate the facts. Fencing is more expensive than in the East, but not a great deal of it is required. A good board fence will cost from one dollar and fifty cents to two dollars per rod. Lumber, such as is used for houses and fencing, costs from twenty-five to thirty-five dollars per thousand. Horses are relatively cheap,—good farm horses bring from twenty-five to seventy-five dollars. Some are much cheaper; but, as they are usually Mexican *broncos*, they might demand the sacrifice of two or three broken necks or limbs before they are tractable enough to be of any satisfactory benefit. I have frequently seen a good horse sell under the hammer for five or ten dollars; but nobody but a native could handle him. Cows bring from twenty-five to forty dollars.

The farmers sow their barley on the 1st of January, and when it ripens they take off a crop of sixty or seventy bushels per acre, and then plant corn, which has abundance of time to mature, and will yield from seventy to eighty bushels per acre. On new land, corn will yield a hundred bushels or more, and barley seventy to the acre. Alfalfa is cut seven or eight times a year, and yields from ten to fifteen tons to the acre. This requires water to produce so much. But water is not wanting. Besides the streams and irrigating canals, there are three hundred artesian wells in San Bernardino Valley.

San Diego County lies immediately south of the counties of San Bernardino and Los Angeles. It forms the southern extremity of the State. It is bounded on the east by Arizona, and on the west it is washed by the sea. Its south line is bounded by Mexico; or, to speak more properly, Lower California. This county has some very prominent features and decidedly desirable points. Take it all and in all, it is not so blessed with advantages as the counties lying immediately upon its north. It has not the agricultural land of Los Angeles, nor the mineral wealth of San Bernardino; and yet it is rich in both. It is preferred by many to either of the counties named. The climate is said to be the best in California. It has not the heat of San Bernardino or Los Angeles, nor the winds or cold of some of the upper sections, nor the enervating influences that are sometimes felt at Santa Barbara. Yet the latter place and San Diego are more nearly alike than any two places in the State, as it regards climate.

The mean temperature of January is about $53°$; of December, $56°$; of July, $70°$; August, $71°$. The mean temperature of the coldest day in the year is about $43°$; the mean temperature of the hottest, $77°$.

The highest range of temperature is about 88°, while the lowest point reached by the mercury is only 33°. The average daily range of temperature is only 12 degrees. Think of that, you who suffer from freezing nights and scorching days. The average rain-fall in San Diego County is from twelve to fifteen inches. And the number of days on which rain falls will not average much more than thirty. And one characteristic of the rain in Southern California is that it more frequently falls in the night.

The variation in the rain-fall is very much greater than in climate, take the entire State together. For the climatic difference between the two extremes of north and south, a distance of nearly a thousand miles, is not so great as one would imagine. Point St. George, in Del Norte County, in the extreme northwest corner of the State, is upon the same isothermal line as Southern Utah. But the rain-fall frequently reaches sixty or seventy inches. San Francisco, situated between the northern and southern extremes, has a rain-fall of nearly twenty inches. It is said that in one year in Klamath County the great quantity of one hundred and twenty-nine inches fell, while at Fort Yuma, in the southeastern extremity of San Diego County, the average annual rain-fall is only about three inches, and sometimes even less. And it is said there are places where no rain falls. The question naturally arises, Why these differences? All the western portion of the continent derives its moisture from the Pacific Ocean. The wind coming off the sea, as it almost invariably does, gathers up the particles of moisture and carries them until some influence causes it to unload its burden.

It is a fact well known that the capacity of atmospheric air to absorb and retain moisture is increased or diminished in proportion as its temperature is higher or lower. The prevailing winds, coming as they do from over the ocean, absorb large quantities of water and carry it along till they become cooled and are obliged to deposit it. In winter, when the sun is south of the equator, the point is reached at about latitude 30°, where the deposition of moisture is begun; and as the winds get cooler in proportion as they get farther and farther away from the heat of the equator and towards the north, the precipitation of moisture increases in a direct ratio with the distance, until by the time Puget Sound is reached the winds are found to be in an almost constant state of precipitation. This deposit is rain in the lowlands and snow upon the mountains.

Of course, in the summer, when the sun is north of the equator, the locality where the cooling process takes place is moved still farther north, so that the places that received rain during the winter receive none during the summer. South of latitude 42° rain in the summer is almost unknown, unless it be in mountain districts, where clouds are attracted and then caused to precipitate their burdens by the cool temperature that is always found in the higher altitudes.

It is naturally supposed that where so little rain falls during the year, as, for instance, in San Diego, the ground must become thoroughly baked and vegetation be destroyed. This, to a very great extent, is true, except where artificial means of irrigation are used.

The reader must remember that in California the seasons are essentially different from what they are in the East. The real winter here is while the heat of the summer months is being endured in the Atlantic States. Stock must be fed in many localities in July and August, just as an Ohio farmer would feed in December. The ground is so thoroughly baked that grasses do not form a sward and spring up from the root afresh each season, as in the East, but reproduce themselves from the seed anew every year. A heavy, soaking rain in California in midsummer would be far more injurious than a drouth in the East.

It is often asked if the great scarcity of rain does not make the dust almost unendurable. In certain localities, where the winds are frequent and strong, the dust is troublesome. But these places are not frequent. As a general thing the dust is thought to be a very small inconvenience.

San Diego County, while it has not so great an area as its neighbor, San Bernardino, is in itself great enough to be sufficient for a principality. The Colorado Desert covers one-third of its surface, and mountains and cañons four millions of acres more, but there are still left two millions of acres suitable for farming and grazing. And the Colorado Desert is such only in name and not in fact; for though it is treeless and arid, its soil is rich, and only requires a bountiful supply of water to make it "blossom as the rose." This supply of water will be forthcoming at some time in the future, for the Gulf of California is higher than a large area of the desert, and it only requires enterprise and money to tap the Gulf, and thus irrigate these parched acres that are so rich.

The agricultural products are very desirable to the county, and indicate the natural advantages of the soil.

An extract from the report of the president of the Chamber of Commerce will give some idea of the resources of this county: "Notwithstanding the drouth of last season, many farmers of this county raised sufficient grain to sow their own fields and a surplus for the market; and to-day we have a larger number of acres under cultivation than ever before, with a better prospect of a large yield. Should the season continue favorable, we will have over one million dollars' worth of wheat alone for foreign markets.

"During the past year a superior quality of granite has been discovered within eleven miles of San Diego. Aside from what has been used in our own city, a large quantity has been shipped to San Francisco, on a contract for one thousand tons. Schooners arriving in our port in future will have no difficulty in obtaining back-freight."

There were exported from San Diego during the year 1873, four years ago, 599,756 pounds of wool, 116,000 pounds of honey, 5344 hides, 40,208 gallons of whale-oil. Since that time the wool and honey exports have about doubled, while other exports have materially increased.

San Diego County, in common with the State, is subject to drouth at intervals of a number of years. But there is no year when the rain-fall in the interior is not sufficient to produce fair crops. An Eastern farmer would soon find here that he would have to change his agricultural tactics to make a success of his business. He must necessarily "discern the signs," for climate, rain-fall, soil, and all must be considered.

If it is thought necessary in the East to plough deep and frequent, it is absolutely more necessary here. For it causes the earth to retain its moisture much longer than when but superficially ploughed.

Ploughing and planting begin in this county in November and continue till about the first of April. And in no part of the United States is a winter and spring view more delightful. The rains give a fresh look to the fields and gardens; and the most beautiful carpet of grass and flowers is to be seen everywhere.

This county furnishes very fine advantages for the agriculturist, pomologist, the herder, and the apiarist,—advantages which, perhaps, cannot be excelled in the State, except in the distance to market. The home consumption of this county is no inconsiderable amount; and then San Diego is not far, as it regards time, from San Francisco, the great market of the entire coast.

I am satisfied that a man with even a small amount of means could, with an apiary and a vegetable-garden, not only make a living but a satisfactory surplus. Bees cost nothing to keep, as flowers are to be found everywhere, at all times of the year. And honey sells readily, right at home, for twenty cents per pound, and commands the highest price both in San Francisco and the East. In 1873 the increase in exportation was one hundred thousand pounds in excess of the preceding year. This county ranks first among the honey-producing counties of the State.

San Diego City is the seat of the county government, and, unlike most towns rapidly built in new countries, has substantial improvements, which indicate enterprise, permanence, and prosperity. Her hotels, churches, banks, private residences, and various artistic improvements would seem to be the work of many years rather than the short period of time in which they have been built. The city is very beautiful, and is a delightful place of residence. The people are refined and intelligent, and have provided ample facilities for improvement and enjoyment, socially, intellectually, and religiously.

There are about three thousand inhabitants in the city, mostly American, who have sought this locality for its health-giving climate and prospects of successful business. The city, and county too, have both,—the former in an eminent degree. But San Diego, while it has fine opportunities, can never become the great commercial centre that its ardent friends anticipate, unless the Southern Pacific Railroad should terminate here, which there is no immediate probability of its doing. San Diego is fixed, by the Texas and Pacific Railroad bill, as the western terminus of the road. This proposed railway is the shortest route over the American continent, connecting the Atlantic, the Gulf of Mexico, and the Valley of the Mississippi with the Pacific.

By comparing a few figures the correctness of the above statement will be seen:

New York to San Francisco, Central route	3283 miles.
New York to San Francisco, Southern route	3359 "
Difference in favor of Central route	76 "
Charleston to San Francisco, Central route	3227 "
Charleston to San Francisco, Southern route	2974 "
Difference in favor of Southern route	253 "
New Orleans to San Francisco, Central route	3107 "
New Orleans to San Francisco, Southern route	2426 "
Difference in favor of Southern route	681 "

It is a very great mistake that the Southern Pacific Railroad has not been built. Here are more than three millions of square miles, denominated the Pacific Coast, that must be reached by one of three ways,—overland teams, by steamer by way of Panama, or by the Union and Central Pacific Railroad. The first is no longer thought of, being wholly impracticable; the second is so repulsive to most people that they would sooner remain East, however inconveniently situated, than bear the sufferings and inconvenience incident to the necessary sea-voyage, preferring "the ills they have, rather than fly to others they know not of." The tariff by the railroad route is necessarily very high. The expense is beyond the means of a large proportion of those who desire to go to California. For the majority of those desiring to make the Golden State their future home are persons of limited means; while rich *tourists* are not very numerous, at least on the Pacific Coast. One hundred and thirty-odd dollars is the fare from New York to San Francisco; and about one hundred and twenty dollars from Cincinnati; one hundred and twenty from Indianapolis; one hundred and sixteen from Chicago; and one hundred from Omaha. These figures are exclusive of meals and sleeping-berths, which will amount to from forty to sixty dollars additional.

Now, any one knows that these figures are too high for the average person desiring to emigrate. If fares could be lower, hundreds would come to this coast where there are but tens now. Whether the railroads can afford to reduce the fares or not, we do not pretend to know.

First-class passage from New York to San Francisco, by steamer or ocean travel by the way of Panama, including berths, provisions, and all, is one hundred dollars. This, to the average emigrant, notwithstanding sea-sickness, is more preferable, but for the time required to make the voyage. One thing Congress should do: it should make an appropriation to the Southern Pacific Railroad, with a provision that the road shall not go into the hands of monopolies without a compensation to Government for assistance rendered. The Pacific Coast and the entire country need three Pacific railroads, at least. The completion of the Southern route will be of inestimable benefit, not only to the millions of inhabitants on the Pacific and Atlantic slopes, but to the Government itself. For it would be a great assistant in opening up the mineral wealth of Arizona and the Indian Territory, besides the agricultural wealth of Texas. Should this road ever be completed it will greatly benefit Southern California,—the very garden of the State,—and San Diego would become a very prominent city, because it has natural advantages that are not found anywhere else on the coast. It has one of the best bays in the world, where the greatest steamers can anchor with perfect safety amidst the severest storm that ever swept the sea.

No part of the State presents a more picturesque appearance than this part of California. The equable character of the temperature during the months of December, January, and February is strikingly expressed in the stagnant condition of many incipient flowers which, having advanced to the character of colored buds, await through these months for warmer days in which to show forth their colors. But it must not be understood that there are no flowers in these winter months. Every day in the year bouquets can be gathered in the open fields.

In sunny nooks in the arroyas is a shrub, apparently an *Erigonum*, which has all through the winter a beautiful, yet small, white flower. There, long weeks before spring has unlocked her frozen doors in the East, the long, green stems of the mandrake (*Cucumis perennis*) begin to trail and display their cluster of beautiful flowers. And at the same time the beautiful purple flowers of the *Alfilerilla* (*Erodium moschatum*), the Spanish clover, so abundant in this section, upon which the cattle fatten. The *Erodium* belongs to the order of geraniums, hence it may truthfully be said that the horses, cattle, and sheep of Southern California feed on geraniums.

At the lowest levels, over which the highest tides flow, *Salsola* and salt grasses appear, and on the clay soil on the elevations the ice-plant (*Mesembryanthemum*) is found. This plant is found occasionally among the mountains. I saw it in the region of the big trees and Yosemite. The leaves are brilliant with saline juices, which give the appearance of ice, whence the name. These are a few of the earliest blooming flowers, but there are myriads of others that do not bloom quite so early, but in early spring cover hill and valley with their variegated hues.

CHAPTER X.

SOCIAL LIFE.

> "But with thyself accompanied, seek'st not
> Social communication."—MILTON.

THERE is no labor to the writer more difficult than to correctly portray the social character of a people. It is, perhaps, doubly so regarding the people of the Pacific Coast. It has been said that it is quite a task to write up the French people, because of their manners, habits, styles, etc. But as they can only be *Frenchy*, however peculiar, it is a comparatively easy task. So it is of any people, civilized or uncivilized, if it be but to write of that people only. But it is wholly different in regard to California.

Take the hundreds of thousands that are around you, the population is cosmopolitan in the most generic sense.

To write up the social life of such a heterogeneous mass would be to treat somewhat upon the social life of the known world. For almost every nation under the sun is represented here, to a greater or less degree, and yet retaining its distinct identity, as far as private habits and customs are concerned.

To be sure, there are statute laws respecting certain acts that govern every person here, but these never touch the individual manners, tastes, etc., of domestic life or religious character.

Then, even the English portion of the inhabitants are from every point whence Englishmen come,—from "stubborn Cornwall" to the American capital. And, of course, each individual thinks his personal habits are the best and wisest. Who ever knew an Englishman, especially an Americanized one, that was not content with the correctness of his own views regarding anything? His tenacity is only equalled by—another English-American. We don't condemn this trait. Who would that understood himself?

This is the character that triumphs when properly directed or circumscribed. It may not always be well directed, but it is as certain to be well circumscribed as that the sun shines when a number of the same blood are together. The hope of the world is that there is more than one person of each nationality.

There is an abundance of this character here— the English—to give general tone to society. Albeit, the Chinese have certainly shaded the question somewhat by their great numbers. But not enough, as we believe, to cause any well-founded panicky feelings.

But, as we have intimated, the cosmopolitan

character of the population is such as to neutralize English social life somewhat.

One feels the strangeness of this phase of life very sensibly when first coming from the semi- or full Puritanic ideas and habits of the East. Yet when you have sufficiently neared the "bed rock" of social life to ascertain correctly what is there, it is found that quite a genuine and strong social element pervades society. Why not? Could it well be otherwise and *be* wise? Purer human nature is found in new rather than in old countries. Don't stand astounded at the assertion; it is *not* used in a moral sense, but simply that you see more clearly human nature as it is, is the idea. Hence new sections always "bear the blame and sport the name" of being very corrupt; whereas they may be but little lower than their old neighbors, only they have less deceit connected with their moral character.

This is especially so of California. While we do not pretend to set up any defence of its moral atmosphere, we must confess that the moral sentiment is not of a very high order; yet, as regards immoral practices in general, they are not worse than in many Eastern States.

Frankness among the masses is very prominent, either in affiliation or non-affiliation.

I was once urged by a prominent gentleman of San Francisco to dine with him, and when I accepted he seemed disappointed and surprised. But he was a new-comer, and never was in his element here. The rule is, if you are invited by a host, you are considered and received, in the fullest sense, as a guest, with a hospitality that would do credit to the kindness and liberality of a Southern host in the balmy days of the "peculiar institution."

It is the natural feeling of the average manly heart. The long stretch of years may have weaned one away from early associations and familiar places of "the long ago," but years never patch over the feeling of comparative isolation.

Eating and drinking are cardinal elements in Pacific Coast life. In many places five meals a day are served; so that one, considering the elongation of each meal, may eat, eat again, and then eat more, from seven in the morning till twelve at night. It is a very Paradise for the appetite, but lamentable on the stomach. Wild and domestic game and the finny gifts of the sea may weight the table in endless profusion, while pastry *de la Paris*, and fruits tropical and semi-tropical, without limit invite you, as the miner has it, "to wade in." Think of grapes rivalling the famous ones of Eschol, and strawberries "the year round," belonging to the esculent branch of social life! while wines, "to the manor made," of every quality for those unfortunate enough to imbibe, are found everywhere, and too often offered.

Social life in general, be it said with sorrow, is not considered "way up," to provincialize a little, or first-class, without the drinks. I once attended a wedding of the daughter of a staid Scotchman. The father entertained me—very interestingly, too, by the way—with his Calvinistic ideas and his knowledge of Scotch divines as long as *ideas were sufficiently clear.* There was the usual variety and amount of provisions for such occasions in this country, while they had wines and brandies in surfeiting quantities: wines in bottles, brandy in pitchers; wines in jugs, and brandies in demijohns; and wines and brandies in all the goblets that I saw; besides "cocktails," "slings," and "punches" *ad libitum.* The word was,—

"On with the dance; let joy be unconfined."

And so it was; and drinks, too, were unconfined. Every one drank and became more or less drunk, but the writer,—especially the *more*, I was persuaded.

Do not gather the idea that this is a land of universal inebriation,—far from it. Amid so much drinking, men can be found who are *Jesuitically* temperate in sentiment and practice. Their efforts and influence are always exerted in the direction of *total abstinence.* And this class is not inconsiderable in number.

Amusements are very numerous,—from a humbugging spiritual séance to a variety troop, or from a first-class lecture to the poorest class theatre. And all are well attended. In some remote places the bull-fight and cock-fight are still indulged in frequently on Sunday, and mainly by the natives, or "greasers," as they are called,—a class having a strong solution of Indian and Mexican blood. Yet such scenes are always witnessed, I am sorry to say, by a greater or less number of American people. Where "troops" or "mediums" are wanting to furnish amusement, often "home talent" is used to fill the deficiency.

This is a land of picnicing and excursions in the summer season. The idea would be correct with the latter part of the sentence left out. For summer, in fact, is not the best time for all out-door amusement. Summer is a favorable time for going to the mountains, or anywhere in the higher altitudes, and hundreds avail themselves of the opportunity. But many are the picnics or short excursions made in midwinter-bay, January or February. Think of it! taking your basket of provisions and luscious fruit and spending a day with a party in out-door rambling in midwinter,—and that, too, amid the wild-flowers!

In some places "accommodations" are not very good, but what odds? I was once invited to join a party for a picnic. I gladly accepted, as I knew nothing of the country, and this afforded me an opportunity for limited observations, at least, having but recently been an "immigrant," as they call every one here who has just arrived from the East.

I adjusted my mind for beautiful groves, green grass, and the songs of birds. I could hardly keep from laughing in my friends' faces when I found we were to picnic under a solitary, dwarfish live-oak-tree,—the only one in the *forest*,—with dead bur-clover and weeds for our grass, and to play croquet in the sun. Of course some localities are better off for shady groves and picnic grounds. I would not have missed this out-door picnic for anything, because it was purely *Californian*, you know.

The old settlers of this State are especially fond of real enjoyment. But some of them, having a matter-of-fact kind of way about them, turn social enjoyment into a practical use. But, why not? Enjoyment is well, but enjoyment with profit is better. I was once stopping in the city of—— No matter,—it was a delightful place. I had barely formed the acquaintance of a gentleman there when he proposed to show me all about the city, but especially was he interested in having me inspect one little vacant lot that backed up the adobe house of one of the natives, who, though humble in appearance, had plenty of money. I found out afterwards that I, being a stranger and inspecting the lot, would probably make the impression that

I desired to purchase, and thus hasten a sale that was hanging wearily between the native and the gentleman with me. But it did not work; the land was not sold, and I was never shown around the city again. My land-speculating friend was never so friendly with me afterwards.

The item to me was a good one, as it illustrates one way of using social life.

By the way, I never saw any place where there was such persistence among real estate agents as in this very city just alluded to. To hear them talk you would think this, and this alone, was the land of everlasting youth so long looked for by Ponce de Leon, and that all these real estate men were better to you and understood your interests better than yourself. They were worse than insurance agents, if possible. Hardly a man could stop in the city a day but it was thought that he certainly did come to buy land, and there was but one piece that would suit him, and each agent had that. He was certain to be entertained, for if he had no acquaintances this class of men would see that he had company, and that nearly all the time.

Of course I did not want to buy real estate. I could not have done so if I had wanted land. But what did that matter? I was a stranger, and that was enough. No man could fathom my intentions or my pocket, hence it was taken for granted that I was a prospective purchaser.

I was shown around the city and country again and again; I was asked by real estate agents to visit different parts till it became monotonous to me. One day an agent, desiring me to visit a piece of land he had for sale, came to me and said, "Can I bore you to-day again?" "If your auger is not too long," I replied. He didn't come for me any more.

The intelligence of the Pacific Coast is above par. There are few families but take the dailies, and in very many instances the literary and scientific monthlies.

Art has a strong hold in the æsthetics of domestic life. Music and painting are very generally cultivated,—more so, by far, than in the older States. But this is not to be wondered at. The grandeur of the scenery and the character of the climate tend to inspire thought and make the spirit vivacious, ready to catch the harmony of sounds, or throw upon the canvas the impress of the scene. What a ridiculous idea is entertained of the mental and social condition of the people upon this coast by many who have never seen them!

A lady once remarked to the writer, "I hardly expected, on arriving here, to find the people so civilized." What could she, or any like her, have thought of a country with such resources and opportunities that demand the best of any people to develop its wealth and power?

And there are tens of thousands in the Eastern States to-day who think that life in the Pacific States is in perpetual peril by wild beasts and savage tribes of Indians, to say nothing of cut-throats, desperadoes, and skulking banditti.

Many a man talks now of the "frontier" as being washed by the waters of the Pacific Ocean, whereas, if that word can be located at all, now, by geographical lines, and if it means a new, undeveloped country, then with very much reason can the Pacific Coast demand that the "frontier line" shall be established for present reference, at least, a thousand or fifteen hundred miles east of the Golden Gate. For in many respects enterprise and improvements are far in advance of the Atlantic or Middle States.

There may be found in all the various avenues of life here alumni from almost all the colleges in this country, and some of the universities of the Old World. It is not a rare matter to see in the cabin when "off shift" a miner amusing himself with the classic literature of Virgil or Homer. If not these, a scientific monthly, or a literary journal of no ordinary character, takes the place.

I remember once of enjoying a hearty dinner and spending a pleasant hour in a cabin, far away from any town or city, with a miner who was an alumnus of Oxford University, England, and whose father enjoys a large salary in the Church of England to-day. His cabin ground, if it was not classic, was literally paved with silver, for he had it paved with stone that would assay four or five hundred dollars to the ton.

The humblest avenues of business sometimes are graced with men who have stood well in the professions.

I once saw a clever lawyer driving a dray, another attending table at a restaurant, another doing duty as a church sexton " on salary." Millionaires are sometimes seen doing the work of the ordinary laborer.

Many recognize the great fact that life is earnest, while some among the rich play the snob and act the boor. But the practical, sensible man goes in the straightest possible line for the greatest success.

A party of tourists—ladies and gentlemen—from the East, visiting the great Bonanza mines not long ago, was by the superintendent taken down the shaft nearly two thousand feet, and shown the manner of working the underground part of mining. It was a rare occasion for the tourists, which few are permitted to enjoy. Upon coming from the shaft one of the most philanthropic, desiring to express his appreciation on behalf of the whole party, gave the superintendent, who was worth a quarter of a million, *fifty cents for his services.*

It is worthy of remark, before we close this chapter, that a man's social relations here may be no indication of the character of his antecedents or former financial standing. Very little hangs on a man's relationship,—he stands for himself.

Some of the strongest moneyed men had very humble beginnings. And more than one that we know of now, who virtually control the money-market of the Pacific Coast, and have the financial destiny of thousands in their hands, were nothing but bar-tenders in low saloons in early days; it is certainly no special credit to their names to-day.

Influences are very positive. A man very soon advances or retrogrades. Good society can be found that refines and elevates, and every individual must be to a degree his own recommendation to it. He who waits for the formal presentations and recommendations of friends finds his desires but partially satisfied. But society is far more willing to receive one into its bosom, frequently, than any careful man should be willing to be received.

The old adage, "think well before you act," is certainly applicable here. We have said there is good society,—so there is, but much of it is like some of the land-titles, you can tell but little about it at first.

Sometimes the general appearance of things is polished and refined, but time and study reveal rottenness and moral stench. I have known men that pass current in society that have a wife and children with them here, and a wife and children they have left in the East. And women who have left their husbands, and sued and obtained divorces because their husbands did not "support them as desired." Of course this is not society, but only exceptions in society. True enough; but it indicates that society, as yet, has not a good moral basis, and that it will bear careful and close study. Upon this very matter are thousands of persons wrecked in this country. And it is wrong not to give persons who design coming to this coast a warning of certain social dangers that are apt to be met.

The marriage relation with many is looked upon as a means of pleasure and convenience, that may be dissolved at pleasure.

I once married a couple who lived together for two weeks and then separated, the reason of which I could never ascertain.

I officiated at the wedding of a very beautiful lady once who seemed to be above the average in intelligence. I learned afterwards that she became acquainted with her husband the same day she was married. I did not think, when I learned the fact, that it was a very good indication of a happy future.

I remember another couple that came to my residence to be united in marriage. The man was a slow, dull fellow, who looked as though he needed some one to take care of him, while the woman was "as sharp as lightning," as they say out in Nevada. I "tied the knot," they asked "the charge," settled the bill, and left under the command of the new wife,—and *parted in two days*. I knew one woman that separated from her husband, married another, and then hired her first husband as a day-laborer.

CHAPTER XI.

THE PEARL OF THE SIERRAS.

"When breezes are soft and skies are fair,
I steal an hour from study and care
And hie me away to the woodland scene."
H. W. BRYANT.

How strange that we are often so sectional in our feelings, sympathies, and observations! Many accounts of localities are more or less *ex parte*, because, unconsciously, the writers are moved by too great a prejudice for or against.

Observations are too frequently made as mere matters of fashion.

Niagara is literally besieged by an army of male and female warriors against wind and weather, not so much because the great falls are so wonderful and unique as from the fact that it is a popular place of resort.

Of course these falls are grand,—they are sublime,—but how few of the tens of thousands of visitors to that resort have been able to describe them, or even felt any inspiration from their sublimity! Like a person of fashion we wot of, who, when he had been admiring the great wonder, suddenly startled the party by the forcible declaration, "It is *pretty*, isn't it?" Thousands do think them *pretty*.

It must not be inferred that we are claiming that visitors should stop visiting Niagara because so few comprehend its greatness, or that none should go but those who do. But we do think there is a semblance of shoddy in the habit of visiting these falls by many because *it is fashionable*, when there is scenery in our country, too, that excels, at any rate equals, the Alpine; and falls, alongside of which Niagara would appear as a chubby infant. Is that overdrawn? Read the facts couched in the chapter on Yosemite.

It is fashionable to go to Long Branch, Saratoga, or what not, but what is the advantage aside from surf-bathing, "drinking the springs," gambling, and taking items of fashion? The former two are no doubt healthful, but the latter are pernicious. The expenditure is too great for the receipts, especially when there is scenery a million times more inspiring, and waters as pure as Saratoga, and certainly farther away from elements of *adulteration;* and surf-bathing can be substituted by purest air and heaven's sunlight at dizzy heights, or amidst enchanting landscapes that no artist's brush can imitate. All this, and infinitely more,—more even than the sensitive, beauty-loving soul can ever fathom,—all for less money than Saratoga or Long Branch pleasures cost for one summer. Yosemite is eminently worthy of all the praise it receives, and more; for as yet it stands, and perhaps will for all time to come, without a rival in kind. But why visit it only, and talk and write only of its beauties, when there are thousands of other objects of interest? And of the many curiosities that nature has scattered over the length and breadth of this coast, Lake Tahoe is one of the most charming.

This is a land of wonders, certainly of curiosities. Providence has made this vast area, between the Rocky Mountains and the sea, his chief receptacle of the wealth of the country. And what folly to travel in foreign countries to see the sights until you have at least seen some of the wonders and treasures of our own great Commonwealth! You can spend your life in exploring these various wonders, and then not find an end,—petrified forests; lost rivers, whose *termini* no one knows, and of whose source there is great doubt; brackish lakes, whose waters are worse than the Dead Sea, and in which no living thing can exist; bubbling, hissing, thundering geysers, whose awfulness impresses the hardest heart; roaring cataracts, that with a band of silver seem to bind together earth and sky; boiling springs, hither and yon in almost countless profusion, that send their breath of steam as through the throats of some great furnace from Vulcan's forge; geographical and topographical features that are marvellous in themselves; the big trees, whose magnitude is a wonder, and whose age links the present almost to the days of Solomon; Yosemite, unlike anything of the kind in the known world, whose sublimity is beyond description; and charming, silvery, unique Tahoe, or Pearl of the Sierras.

There is no patent on the name, hence we have chosen to christen it thus.

And who will say it is a misnomer that has seen its grandeur and enjoyed the beauty of its surroundings?

Its name belongs to the Indian tongue, and signifies *clear water*.

This lake in its greatest length is twenty-three miles, and greatest width eleven miles; hence it has an area of two hundred and fifty-three square miles. Its altitude is six thousand two hundred and twenty feet above the level of the sea. Here, spread out before me, like the finest of burnished silver, is a lake unlike any other body of water in the world, save one in Switzerland, and that has only a few marks of similarity.

This lies nestled away, like a very jewel, in the summit of the Sierras,—the Alps of America,—at an altitude of a mile and a quarter above the level of the sea. Think of it! A body of water containing an area of more than two hundred and fifty square miles, and deep enough to float the largest vessel that ever traversed the sea, and then have almost immeasurable depths below the keel; think of this being in the very summit of the greatest range of mountains in America!

It has been sounded along the line between Nevada and California, which runs through the lake, to the distance of two hundred and fifty-three fathoms, or fifteen hundred and eighteen feet. But other places have been sounded to the great distance of nearly twenty-five hundred feet. The character of the water is almost incredible to one who has never looked upon it. Coming down from the springs that burst from the cañons, and the everlasting snows that crown the mountain-tops, where

> "'Tis the felt presence of the Deity,"

the water is almost perfectly pure.

I have leaned over the side of the boat and watched the play of the trout a *hundred and fifty feet* below the surface. I have dropped a small, shining, metallic button, and watched distinctly its oscillations in sinking for three or four minutes.

The transparent nature of the water is best seen in the morning, when the lake is perfectly calm; not even the small surface ripples that nearly always exist on ordinary streams and lakes are visible.

The various angles of vision present the most charming scene. Yonder the lake looks like a quiet mass of molten silver; yonder, where the rays of the sun meet you, is a gorgeous array of crimson and gold; then there is a range of purest emerald, deepening into blue-black as the scene stretches away from you, bespangled in the distance by the rising white-caps. This, fringed with the green of the deep pine-forests that skirt the mountains and capped with the everlasting snows, made radiant with the flood of sunlight, furnishes a picture of incomparable beauty, and worthy of a master's brush.

But here by you, right at your feet, is one of the most pleasing features of all: so still in the morning quietness, and such air-like purity withal. You think you can reach down and pick up those shining pebbles, and yet they are twenty, thirty, or forty feet beneath you. And that boat or skiff seems to be poised in mid-air. You can count the small indentures and nail-heads in the very keel.

You cringe with fear as your boat glides towards that huge bowlder, as large as a church, thinking surely your vessel will be wrecked; but there is no danger, as the rock is many feet beneath you. The transparency of the water makes the danger seem so near.

How often have I wished this place—mountains, lake, and all—could be the place of one of the grand Eastern camp-meetings! This bracing air, this unique spot, this wonderful lake, this rich, healthful aroma of deep pine-forests, this grand scenery, all combined, make it one of the best of places for religious summer resort.

Yonder is a quaint spot, a veritable Gibraltar on a small scale, a lonely, rocky island in the centre of Emerald Bay. Some foolish man built a tomb in the solid rock on its summit, intending to be buried there, where the marks of decay come slowly over his grave, and where he might sleep undisturbed amid the incomparable grandeur that would have surrounded him. His sarcophagus and all were prepared, but the treacherous billows of the lake, that occasionally foam and roar with fury, seized him, and he lies buried at the bottom,—no man knows where, for no one going down ever comes up again from these waters.

CHAPTER XII.

SUMMERING AT LAKE TAHOE.

"How pure its waters! its shallows are bright
With colored pebbles and sparkles of light;
And clear the depths where its eddies play,
And dimples deepen and whirl away."—BRYANT.

"Gorgeous was the time,
Yet brief as gorgeous."—MRS. SIGOURNEY.

IT was first an artless, genial party of three of us that drank in the poetry of the scenery around Lake Tahoe. The "elect lady," whose presence has ever been an inspiration and encouragement in life's blackest, bitterest hours, her best and dearest friend, Miss Torreyson, and the writer, made up the trio. We were joined by and by with a party of others kindred in spirit, who entered into all our schemes and reconnoissances after pleasure.

Those were memorable six weeks; and now, at this distance of many months on the road of time, that period of frolic and recuperation gleams as with the radiance of youth's happiest sunset scene. How strange that happy days even never look so charming as when they are mellowed in the deep past!

> "Strange we never prize the music
> Till the sweet-voiced bird has flown;
> Strange that we should slight the violets
> Till the lovely flowers are gone."

If the present should shine as brightly as the sheen of past pleasures, we would ever be struggling to fasten the hand of time that it might not move.

During the days we enlivened many a bright morning hour with boat-riding, fishing, gathering wild-flowers, and such other amusements as this delightful place afforded. On one of these fishing excursions one of our party came very near falling into the treacherous waters of the lake.

Our favorite resorts, and it is so with all tourists, were Emerald and Carnelian Bays. The former is a beautiful, land-locked arm of the lake, walled in by rugged and towering cliffs. The latter is a long, gravelly beach, where by the hour we have searched for carnelian stones, of which some of the purest quality are found.

The mountains and cañons are most delightful points of interest as places of observation and rest, and often charm by the echoes they throw back. We were given to song; and many a time summering here, and travelling over the lake, we united in singing the "Evergreen Mountains of Life" and "A Thousand Years," our favorite lake airs; the former suggested, no doubt, by the towering mountains that surrounded us. The effect is peculiarly fascinating, as the song rings out over the waters, in the pure mountain air, and echoing dies away, after many reverberations of "evergreen mountains of life"—"mountains of life"—"life"—in some deep cañon. Or "a thousand years, Columbia,"—"years, Columbia,"—"Columbia,"—the vowels of the last becoming beautifully distinct in the echoes.

Nearly south of the head of Lake Tahoe, a distance of perhaps a mile and a half, is a little lake that bears the name of Fallen Leaf; and then to the west of this some three miles is Cascade Lake, as charming a little body of water as ever flashed back the sunlight. Of all the objects of interest here, none of its kind is more interesting than this delightful lake, that spreads itself out a half-mile by a mile and a half, and that at an altitude of four or five hundred feet above Tahoe.

Above this, from the summit of Tallac Mountain, it is positively asserted *seventeen* lakes, varying in size, can be seen at one glance nestled away like a cluster of diamonds in the bosom of the Sierras. All these lakes abound with the finest of trout, and are surrounded by the best of game.

On the east side of Tahoe are Cave Rock and Shakspeare Rock. The former is a bald precipitous peak, that presses its perpendicular side almost to the water's edge, leaving just room enough for the road of the old overland stage-coach. Under this rock is a cave of small pretensions, but with the wild scenery, the bald, dizzy height of the cliff, and the fine view of the lake, it is one of the many frequented places.

Shakspeare Rock stands back perhaps full half a mile from the landing at Pray's Bay, or Glenbrook. It is a perpendicular cliff of well on towards a thousand feet above the waters of the lake. It has its name from a well-defined portrait of a man, moss-formed or wind-chiselled, doubtless, that is seen plainly several hundred feet up the rugged side. It is said to look very much like the old bard of Stratford-upon-Avon. But of this we cannot say; we never saw him.

It was on one of Nature's brightest days that our trio, lunch-armed, toiled up its rugged side, the only accessible point, and flung our handkerchief banners to the breeze from the improvised flag-staff, while we grew enraptured at the rich perspective from the dizzy height.

It seemed almost like being on "cloud's rest" as some cloud's shadow fell upon us while there.

Below us lay the bustling, thriving village of Glenbrook, having, perhaps, well on towards a thousand souls as the number of its inhabitants; increased by tourists, and, of course, largely diminished in the winter months, when business here "shuts down." The temperature, however, is generally fine from the last of April to the first of November, or even later. It is not unpleasant now, as I write,—the middle day of January,—to be out boat-riding or rambling by the shore.

This is the outlet of the entire lake and its surroundings; an immense traffic in lumber, etc., is carried on. Five saw-mills give life and activity to the place, as they cut nearly three hundred thousand feet per day, or more than fifty millions during the business months of the year. A hotel, store, post-office, with daily mail, and telegraph-office, add to the convenience of the place.

There are six steamers on the lake that run for pleasure-parties and traffic.

From the lake one of the most unique railroads ever built runs to the summit, a distance of nine miles by the route travelled, although the distance by an air line is but three, while the elevation that it gains is eight hundred and fifty feet. It climbs the mountain by zigzag movements, like a letter Z, the engine sometimes hauling its burden, and sometimes pushing the train. More than a quarter of a million of dollars were required to build and stock this novel short line. It is a rare evidence of engineering skill, and certainly is a good illustration of Western enterprise. It lacks at least a dozen miles of connecting with any other railroad point, and its engines, rolling-stock, etc., had to be hauled up the mountain eight thousand feet high.

This chapter would be incomplete did we not refer to the gentleman who has done so much for the business around the lake, and the comfort of tourists who come; we refer to Captain A. W. Pray. He is a native of Maine, where it is said they "plant school-houses and raise men." He was born September 6, 1820. For many years he was master of a vessel upon the Atlantic Coast. He emigrated to California, we believe, in 1853. He followed his sea-faring business for a number of years after coming to the Pacific, and was master of a vessel that ran up the coast as far as Puget Sound.

Some dozen or so years ago the captain came into possession of vast tracts of timber and arable lands that really hold the key to the lake. He has kept adding piece to piece, till more than four thousand acres of the best land that lies about the lake are in his possession. Nor is his money stingily hoarded. Public institutions of a beneficial sort, charity, churches, worthy enterprises, the needy, are sure to find assistance in Captain Pray. His liberality nearly reaches to a fault. But his liberal spirit is never extended toward an unworthy object. No man more positively repels the idea of giving to or countenancing the worthless and debauched than he. He is a most uncompromising temperance man. Having control of nearly all the town of Glenbrook, there is not a drop of ardent spirits allowed to be sold. He could receive the highest rents for houses for saloon purposes, but would rather lose money than make it by such means. His standard of temperance is not greater than that of his morals. No man is more circumspect in his dealings and actions before men than he. His summer residence is always open to his friends at Tahoe. And many a time have we seen it almost filled with those that were only acquaintances rather than intimate friends that he chose to entertain.

Once I knew the captain to threaten to discharge one of his hired men for using profane language, and would have done so but for the faithful promises that it would not be repeated. In this land of Sabbath-breaking no business whatever is carried on on Sunday where he has control.

It is worthy of remark that the captain is ignorant of these items that we have given of him. But it affords us pleasure to bear evidence to so true a man and so good a character. There is a fashion on this coast of puffing the most shoddy and despicable individual if he but have money, and almost entirely ignoring the true and the good who do not choose to pay for notices. Recognizing this, we have made this notice of a worthy man " without money and without price."

CHAPTER XIII.

TOWARDS YOSEMITE.

> " And there are mem'ries rushing o'er
>   My awe-struck soul to-night,
> Of pleasures that may come no more,
>   Of blossoms hung with blight;
> Of sunny skies whose smiling blue
>   Looked down on plains of bloom;
> Of happy homes that quickly flew
>   On wings of joy's perfume."

"HAVE you visited *the Valley* yet?" is a question that the tourist may prepare himself to answer at least a thousand times. And the question is framed as though the speaker would be surprised if you even inquired what valley was meant. There are hundreds of valleys, big and little, in California, but none that has received the liberal *sobriquet* of "*the Valley*" except that incomparable natural wonder, Yosemite (pronounced Yo-semity).

Whatever may be seen in this realm of sights and things, one entire chapter is left out of memory's book if Yosemite is omitted. As far as observation is concerned, it were better to omit a visit to all the rest of the wonders of the State than to this indescribable realm of sublimity. But let us not premeditate.

It was a little late in the season when our party, equipped for the wearisome journey, turned our faces towards this valley, which is about one hundred and fifty miles east of San Francisco,—that is, in a straight line. But by any road that can be travelled the distance is not short of two hundred and fifty miles. This is no great length to travel, one would think, especially when one hundred miles of it are by palace car, and nearly as many more by stage-coach. Rev. T. Dewitt Talmage cautioned the writer that this two hundred and fifty miles were more fatiguing than the entire trip from New York to San Francisco. And so we thought by the time we had completed it. Ours was, in the main, a genial party, whose hearts had opened to each other somewhat as we crossed the continent. We were entire strangers up to the present journey, which began in the East. Most people are sensible enough to be natural when travelling, hence a person may, with a good deal of safety, after observing his fellow-travellers for a few days, select from the number some whose acquaintance will be profitable. And kindred spirits always attract each other, so that the various little excursions are generally very pleasant.

This was the case with our party of a third of a hundred, with the exception of two or three persons, and each of these "was a party by himself." So they disturbed no one as much as themselves.

It was four P.M. towards the last of July, when we left the freezing winds of San Francisco for the train at Oakland wharf. What marked changes there are here in the temperature in a little distance! How we shivered and slandered the cold of the city on this midsummer's day, and then a fifteen minutes' ride across the bay to the latter city changed our shivering to fans and linen coats and sweat!

It is just a hundred miles to Lathrop, where we changed cars for Modesto, at which place ended our evening journey, and where our wearing, hard travel began next morning. The road we travelled lay through some of the richest country in California, until we reached the Coast Range of mountains, after passing which we travelled through a part of the San Joaquin Valley.

Here was pointed out to us the mirage, that queer atmospheric freak that taught us that

> "There is room for vast deception"

in these beautiful plains.

Many sad, weird stories are told of the fatal deceit of the mirage in early days. The parched plains, in midsummer, spread out as far as the eye could reach before the weary, foot-sore traveller. Man and beast had struggled for months across the plains to the land of gold. Death had stopped the caravan occasionally to claim a victim; disease had perhaps been an ever-present enemy; but on they travel. Hope was anchored to that within the newly-discovered Eldorado. The savages of the West disputed the advance; famine from exhausted provisions was but a worse foe. And long wastes must be crossed with indescribable thirst, often, from the lack of water, but on they travel. Thirst increases; the bloodshot eye and look of despair of the emigrant, and the lowing of the cattle, told plainly of the suffering. A halt was certain death; to travel on could not be worse. Every thought and dream were of water; every change in the contour of the plain would revive hope that water was near. Sometimes, when the travellers would be in just such condition, in the distance would appear the most beautiful lake of crystal water, reflecting the clouds or sky, and fringed by inviting trees of shade. Beasts would catch the sight and seem to quicken speed, while flagging spirits would revive, and fathers would encourage their despairing wives and cheer weeping children. Yonder is the water in full view. The caravan presses onward; it still lies temptingly in the distance. An hour passes; the lake is there, but is no nearer. Hour after hour wearily goes by, and thirst becomes an inward, devouring fire,—but there lies the inviting water. One becomes a raving maniac, and with swollen tongue soon dies. Then another and another and another.

And the faithful ox that has been true so long and so far drops exhausted; then another and another, till man and beast,—till father and mother and child,—on the very verge of the land they longed for so much, suffer an indescribable death, lured away and deceived by the treacherous mirage.

I looked out of the car-window. There it was, "as of yore," spread far out in the distance before us. The most beautifully appearing stream, and such inviting shade upon its banks! I could hardly believe it when I was told it was a deception. I could readily see how a thirsty traveller could be enticed away to death. Where this was pointed out to us there was but little or no water at all.

In this valley, up to where night shut down on us, the land is generally more or less impregnated with alkali, so that farm products, such as wheat and hay, were comparatively meagre.

At this point—Modesto—began both our interest and fatigue. Here was the beginning of a stage-trip of ninety miles, all to be accomplished in twelve hours, over a plain where the heat was stifling and the dust blinding. Only once or twice during the entire journey did we get a sight of water, except at the wells where the horses were watered. We crossed the Merced River, and one or two depressions where there is a mere semblance of a stream in the rainy season. The

Merced is a stream of considerable water. It was necessary to patronize the dilapidated old ferry-boat to get the stages across. The propelling power was by the boatman's arms pulling at a rope that was stretched across the river and fastened on each shore. We travelled the entire forenoon in a continuous body of wheat that was "white to the harvest."

The parched ground, that had not felt the soothing kiss of rain for many, many weeks, and the dead-ripe grain that surrounded us everywhere, reflected the heat so that it became oppressive. And the dust rose in clouds around us, and then travelled as we travelled, for there was not breeze enough to drive it ahead of us, nor did we go fast enough to leave it behind.

Miss K——, who had in the morning demanded with her own peculiar emphasis an outside seat upon the stage, now found—when it was too late to change, and nobody was disposed to accommodate her—that her zeal and selfishness had misled her, for she got all the dust, no shade, and her face was burned to a blister. But as she had been all the while a "party by herself," so nobody cared.

The great want of this valley is water. The quality of its soil is very superior, save here and there where it is strongly impregnated with alkali. This difficulty is now being met somewhat by the cultivation of the sugar-beet, which in a measure destroys the alkali. These beets possess eight per cent. of clarified sugar. They are very profitable, for the yield is enormous.

This beet produces from twenty to thirty tons per acre, and would yield twice as much if allowed to grow. The amount of saccharine matter is much greater if the beets are not allowed to become too large.

The mangel-wurzel beet produces frequently eighty tons per acre. These sell at from three to four dollars per ton. The sugar-beets command a better price.

Lands in the San Joaquin Valley can frequently be purchased at low prices. But it is a question whether cheapness is economy, as many of these lands, such as can be bought at a low figure, are frequently unproductive, although having good soil, for the want of irrigation. However, wells can be sunk, and wind-mills—such as are used all over the State—erected, that will furnish water enough to irrigate large tracts of lands. But considerable expense attaches to this improvement.

At about one P.M. we left the valley and entered the outer foot-hills of the Sierra Mountains, following the general direction of the Merced River. This stream has its source absolutely in Yosemite Valley, although it is formed of all the waters pouring into that great chasm from Lake Tenaya to Bridal-Veil Falls.

We passed, in the afternoon, Bear Valley, a village of three or four houses and a saloon, situated in the Fremont claim. This was a Mexican grant that was purchased by General Fremont, and it covers all the more valuable portion of the county. It includes about ten square leagues, or forty-four thousand three hundred and eighty-six acres. Great mining interests lie in this claim, but are not yielding much now. Occasionally we saw Chinamen placer-mining along the ravines.

Late in the evening we passed through Mariposa, where we changed our coaches for light open wagons, as with these we could better climb the mountains, that were now getting very steep, than with the heavy stages. We soon passed fearful chasms and precipitous places. One evening late we were driving very rapidly along one of these places when the wheel of the wagon I chanced to be in struck a stone, throwing me entirely out of the vehicle and near the edge of one of these fearful precipices.

White & Hatch's hotel was reached by us in the evening at a late hour, after a most wearisome journey. This was but twelve miles from Clark's, from which we made our detour to the famous Big Trees. What delightful retreats these mountain hotels are! And, in fact, all the homes in California, unless it be the lowest hovel, have an air of comfort about them that is not seen, as a

HUTCHING'S HOTEL.—YOSEMITE VALLEY.

rule, in the East. They believe here in having a comfortable, cozy home, if they have nothing else in the world. And the laws are framed to that end,—they protect and guarantee the homestead. I do not think the law is altogether a wise one. In Nevada it is possible for a person to break up, owing his creditors any sum of money, and he himself have many thousands of dollars in a homestead. And the law protects him.

Money has always been plenty in this country, and the idea prevailed that one of the main features of domestic life was to have a cozy, comfortable home. And so it was, and is. It need not be grand. And let it be ever so small, but have it pleasant and comfortable. I have seen the finest Brussels carpet on a cabin of one room. I do not now remember of a house in all the range of my travels on the Pacific Coast, unless it be a Chinaman's hut, a miner's cabin, or a bachelor's retreat, that had not a good showing of carpets and other comforts. I have seen, far away from railroads, and cities, and even out of range of any settled neighborhood, small cabins that were finely furnished. One we passed on this weary trip, on the lower edge of San Joaquin Valley, many miles from any neighbor,—a little cabin of one room that was most cozily furnished, and as inviting as many an aristocrat's drawing-room. I have seen the walks and cobblings in the yards fronting houses made of stone that would assay a hundred dollars per ton. Do not mark this as a great freak of extravagance. This stone would not pay to "work" as ore, but it did make very fine walks. And the furnishing of the houses as stated was a mere outcropping of good sense, for it certainly greatly added to the enjoyments of life.

These hotels where we dine and lodge, although scores of miles from railroads, amidst mountains, and accessible only by rugged roads, and far from any habitation, spread inviting tables, with not only the necessaries, but luxuries, for the appetite. And the only transportation for these articles often is the pack-mule. The rooms are clean and neatly furnished, and would do credit to the hotels of more pretentious cities. Aside from the isolation of society, a whole season at these mountain homes would be a delightful recreation. Nature's grandest scenery surrounds them, the most invigorating air fills the lungs, and makes music through the deep forest.

Never did earth present a more enchanted spot since

"Childhood's sunny hours"

than White & Hatch's at the end of that hard day's stage ride. And never was sleep a more welcome visitor. With an emphasis never before so strong could we utter, as we threw ourselves on the snow-white couch,—

> "Tired Nature's sweet restorer,
> Balmy sleep."

And so we realized it, for the morning found us refreshed, but muscle-sore.

Here began the *big trees*, but not the famous ones, *sui generis*, of which the world has heard so much and yet knows so little. For how can any one in type give the proper idea of these giants, when a whole day's stay among them but develops the idea of their greatness that never seems to become perfect?

Here is an immense forest of pine-trees, through which we travel for miles before reaching Clark's hotel, that are themselves very large. It is not an uncommon thing to see trees whose diameter is from ten to fourteen feet. And these stand thickly upon the ground.

I noticed in this forest, in certain localities, many trees whose lower limbs were covered with long, shaggy moss, of a light-green color, forming a beautiful fringe to the boughs. We gathered here a souvenir for our cabinet.

A few hours' rest, and a luscious dinner,—good enough for a king,—to which we did ample justice, for our ride in these mountain regions had aroused our appetites, gave us fine spirits for an afternoon visit to the great wonders of the forest,—the Big Trees.

When these trees were discovered, they gave an

unexpected task to the botanist to determine just their position in the vegetable world. As none had ever been seen before, and these were unlike any other trees, it was decided that these were *sui generis*. But a name for them,—that was the puzzling question. The English botanists, desiring to show their appreciation of their great duke, dubbed them *Wellingtonia*, which was about as sensible as if they called them *Elephantine*, *Samsonian*, or some such appellation. However, we have done no more wisely, for we have Americanized the name and called them *Sequoia gigantea*. The latter name is well enough, for it certainly conveys a correct idea of these giants. But *Sequoia* is nothing but the name of an Indian chief, the meaning of which will never be known. And it perhaps has no more relation to the nature of these trees than it has to the wind that sighs through their branches.

Here was to commence an entirely new and interesting feature of our whole tour. We were to change the stage and hack for the horse and mule. It was an interesting occasion when the animals were brought to the front, for a wanton selfishness was now manifested as it had not hitherto been.

And the idea, too, was a ludicrous one, that there should be any choice among these forlorn animals. Poor brutes! how I pitied them! Bones covered with skins, having a little of that something called *life*,—and not much of that,—were all these animals were. Subsistence for man had to be carried on pack-mules, and there was no excess of transportation for provender for the animals, except now and then as a rare chance was afforded. These animals, from forty to fifty of them, subsisted on what grass they could find in the ravines, and browsing on the bushes. There could be but little choice, except in shades of color or the length of the animals' ears.

Two objections, at once, were raised by the ladies of our party. Donkeys were preferable to the horses, as they were in better condition, being hardier beasts, and the ladies must take them or fare worse, but a good deal of hesitancy was manifested before mounting the mules. And then, all must be on a level in mode of travel, as "necessity knows no law," hence they rode *more hominum*, a sensible style in these groves or even in crowded cities. The most graceful and easy horsemen in the world are those that sit astride. Here in these narrow trails and steep pathways common sense is forced to break away from the iron rule of custom, and look first to comfort and safety.

Our grotesque appearance,

> "Or witty joke our airy senses move
> To pleasant laughter."

And why not, with such a cavalcade? Such queer

costumes and ways of travel not known before! It was never thought to veil the eye or primp the face, much less that

> "Scaly gauntlet now, with joints of steel,
> Must glove the hand."

for it was nature's unfamiliar realm, and *coarser* objects, humanly speaking, that we were now to visit. We could not but travel " Indian fashion,"— single file,—for road-masters have never expended much on highways. We were more than four thousand feet above sea-level when we mounted these noble (?) brutes, but now we were ascending at every step, and must continue to do so for more than two thousand feet additional. The rugged snow-capped mountains that surround us, and occasionally bare their rocky sides to the view, and the melancholy sough of the wind as it plays among these monarchs of the forest, give an awe to the feelings and a grandeur to the scene that is not found except in like places. The loneliness is very impressive; the perspective adds to it, and the moaning of the wind, the only sound heard, save the talk of your own party, but increases the feeling. Not a bird, whose warble would be company, nor an animal, but your faithful horse, the sight of which would break the monotony, is seen. There is game in these mountains,—the grizzly bear, the lion, deer, and others; but they love the pleasure of solitude, and rarely come where man can, with them, dispute possession. One feels here his own weakness and littleness, and intuitively he mutters, "The Lord God omnipotent reigneth."

The Big Trees, as they are technically called, are of a light, bright cinnamon color, and have a diameter at the ground of from twenty-five to forty feet, a height of from three hundred to four hundred and fifty feet, and a bark that will average one foot and a half in thickness where it has not been molested. I have seen blocks of bark that would measure thirty-two inches in thickness, and I have no doubt but some trees have bark that would average nearly three feet. The texture is loose and spongy, and when cut transversely it is often worked into pincushions and such like toys. The wood is light as the cedar, but is susceptible of a very fine polish. I had a cane made from a piece that I bought of the guide, and I found it would polish equal to mahogany. The Mariposa grove is a State park, together with Yosemite Valley, given by the United States government.

This grove, "together with the Yosemite Valley with its branches and spurs, an estimated length of fifteen miles, and in average width one mile back from the edge of the precipice on each side of the valley, with the stipulation, nevertheless, that the State shall accept this grant on the express condition that the premises shall be held for public use and recreation, and shall be inalienable for all time." So it is absolutely impossible to get a bit of bark or piece of wood except from the guide, who is allowed to gather them from the outskirts of the grove from a tree that has fallen or one that stands outside of the prescribed limits.

There has but one fallen, however, since their discovery, and that was felled by men's hands. It was done by immense augers. It took five men twenty-two days to fell the tree, equal to the services of one man for *one hundred and ten days*. Think of that,—nearly four months' work, not counting any time lost by Sundays, or rainy days, or sickness, to fell one tree! That tree would have yielded more than a thousand cords of four-foot wood and a hundred cords of bark, more than eleven hundred cords altogether. On the stump of this tree there is a house—"whose foundation is sure"—thirty feet in diameter. This house contains room enough in square feet, if it were the right shape, for a parlor twelve by sixteen, a dining-room ten by twelve, a kitchen ten by twelve, two bedrooms ten feet square each, a pantry four by eight feet, two clothes-presses one and a half feet deep and four feet wide, and still have a little to spare.

The foliage of these trees resembles the cedar somewhat. They bear a cone not more than two inches in length, and a black pitch bitter as gall.

The forests at present have a gloomy appearance, as some time in the past, no one knows when, the Indians, the better to facilitate their hunting, burned off the chaparral and rubbish, and, as a matter of course, disfigured the trees by burning off nearly all the bark.

The first sight of these monarchs is one of sore disappointment. For you have travelled many miles where the trees are all large, and here, surrounded as they are by immense pines, their magnitude is not appreciated. But their greatness grows very rapidly upon you, so that if there was at first disappointment, there is now a greater awe. Our first view of interest was the Fallen Monarch, a ponderous old trunk stretched out upon the ground for more than two hundred feet, upon which a stage and four horses could be driven with ease. We had to go a hundred feet towards the top to climb upon the trunk. The diameter of this tree, without bark, at the base is twenty-two feet, one hundred feet from the root it is twelve feet.

How long this monarch has been sleeping no one pretends to know.

The guide says it is no more decayed now, to all appearances, than it was when first discovered. The tree of greatest interest is the Grizzly Giant, which has an altitude of more than three hundred feet. The first thing we did to try its magnitude was to surround it on horseback, passing around in single file, the head of one horse to the tail of another. It called into requisition twenty-five horses out of the twenty-eight in our party to complete the measurement.

This is not considered strictly correct, mathematically speaking, but it indicates the size of the tree by *horse measurement*.

I had prepared myself with a good-sized string, and, with the help of a friend, made close calculation four feet from the ground, and found it to be ninety-three feet, giving a diameter of thirty-one feet. This tree has a limb one hundred feet from the ground that is six feet in diameter. These trees stand around us in quiet grandeur, but to write of one is to write of many, hence the reader must not be wearied with a notice of each. Pluto's Chimney is a hollow tree, standing upright, into which several of us rode on horseback. Yonder is another that had fallen in some past age, and sixty feet or more of it had burned from the root upward, and then toward the top had burned in two, leaving a barrel-shaped or hollow part of the trunk some fifty feet in length. Through this we all rode without any inconvenience. I have understood that several have ridden abreast through it, which I do not think improbable.

This completed our tour among these forest giants. There are two groves—and, properly speaking, but two—of these *Sequoia gigantea*, the

"THE MOTHER OF THE FOREST"—CALAVERAS GROVE.

Mariposa and Calaveras groves. The first is about twenty miles south of Yosemite Valley, perhaps a little more, while the latter is some fifty miles northwest of the valley. Thus it will be seen that they are not, as many suppose, in the great Yosemite Valley.

The big trees of California, not of this species, however, are not confined to these two groves. Many of the noted redwood species (*Sequoia sempervirens*) used to grow back of Santa Cruz, many of which are standing yet that were very great in size. We once upon a time, with five others, rode into one of these during a storm. The butt was hollow, and large enough to hold at least twelve men on horseback, and was not less than two hundred and fifty feet in height.

Never will we forget our ramble among these forests. The effect will remain with memory while it shall last.

Our feeling, as we left them, was one of silent reverie, and adoration to Him who gave such evidences of His creative power.

"The giant trees in silent majesty,
Like pillars stand 'neath heaven's mighty dome:
'Twould seem that perched upon their topmost branch,
With outstretched finger, man might touch the stars;
Yet could he gain that height, the boundless sky
Were still as far beyond his utmost reach
As from the burrowing toilers in a mine.
Their age unknown, into what depths of time

Might Fancy wander sportively, and deem
Some Monarch Father of this grove sent forth
His tiny shoot when the primeval flood
Receded from the old and changèd earth.
Perhaps coeval with Assyrian kings
His branches in dominion spread; from age
To age his sapling heirs with empires grew.
When Time those patriarchs' leafy tresses strewed
Upon the earth, while Art and Science slept,
And ruthless hordes drove back Improvement's stream,
Their sturdy oaklings throve, and in their turn
Rose when Columbus gave to Spain a world.
How many races, savage or refined,
Have dwelt beneath their shelter! Who shall say
(If hands irreverent molest them not)
But they may shadow mighty cities, reared
E'en at their roots, in centuries to come,
Till with the 'Everlasting Hills' they bow,
When 'Time shall be no longer!'"

CHAPTER XIV.

YOSEMITE.

"Its bounding crystal frolick'd in the ray,
And gushed from cleft to crag with saltless spray."
BYRON'S *Island*.

"Life, so varied, hath more loveliness
In one brief day than has a creeping century
Of sameness."—BAILEY'S *Festus*.

"Go abroad
Upon the paths of Nature, and when all
Its voices whisper, and its silent things
Are breathing the deep beauty of the world,
Kneel at its simple altar, and the God
Who hath the living waters shall be there."
N. P. WILLIS.

IT is said that there's a time when "two are company but three are none." So there may be a similar experience even among tourists. A gentleman, his wife, and myself found that three *would* be a company, and that in some respects twenty or thirty were too many. So we hired an extra guide for our special accommodation, and moved several hours in advance of the party. There was no danger from Indians, and the wild beasts of these mountains have no desire to attack travellers if travellers do not attack them, hence there was no danger to us for want of numbers.

Our main motive in being renegades from our party, whom we have never met since, was to abbreviate the time for our journey. We had common feelings in many respects, for we alike were pressed for time. As it was, my friends were the sad losers, even in the time given, for their bright little babe died in their Eastern home while we were at the valley. It is unfortunate to have to hurry through these sublime scenes, for one never sees them but once, in all probability.

Before the sun began to light even the highest peaks of the mountains "round about" us, and while the rest of our party, whom we were forsaking, were still asleep, our quartet party was in the saddle, with faces turned northward towards one of the world's greatest wonders, which millions have longed to see, and seeing which one can never forget,—Yosemite. The air was sharp and bracing, although but the latter part of July, and as clear and pure as ether. Wraps were brought into requisition in the first hour of our morning ride, for an altitude of four thousand feet in the mountains, where snow seldom entirely disappears from the highest points, never gets uncomfortably warm; besides, we were to ascend much of the way.

The poesy, for such we choose to call it, of an early ride amid scenery such as lay around us, will never be forgotten. We had hardly fairly started from Clark's hotel, where we had spent the night after visiting the Big Trees, before we crossed a delightful mountain stream whose " waters were clear as crystal," and whose murmuring over the rocky bottom was a soothing lullaby to our sleeping comrades behind. We were pleased when our horses were presented to find we had a change from yesterday. But if we had painful sympathy then we have a bitter anguish now, for we had gone but a short distance before we found we must carefully economize horse strength or else we should have to depend upon the resources Nature gave us for transportation.

Our guide was an old miner and mountaineer, who had had long experience in these remote quarters. He was very communicative, and seemed to have some idea of almost anything connected with the sights and things we were desiring to see. How much truth was connected with many of his sayings we had no means of determining. He had a dog that was his constant companion; and while he did not talk so much as his master, upon some things he appeared as well informed. He obeyed orders given him with as much promptness as a child. To show the intelligence of this dog the guide dropped his hat, and rode on perhaps a mile. Then calling his dumb servant, he gave him to understand what had occurred, and directed him to "hurry and find" the lost article. Without waiting for further orders, he put off at full speed, while we allowed our jaded animals to rest. In a short time the dog came back with the hat, which he lay at his master's feet. This gentleman and his dog were once connected with a surveying-party in these mountains. Through carelessness or accident the book in which the calculations were kept was lost. Of course this was a serious misfortune, for all previous work without it was of no value. Hour after hour was spent by the entire party in looking for the lost book, but to no advantage. The search was about to be abandoned, when this same dog's master acquainted him with the facts, and ordered him to find the book, which he did in a short time.

Our guide had a miserable horse, which compelled him to remain in the rear a good deal of the time. When he did he gave his dog orders to act as director, which he did very satisfactorily.

There are a great many of these faithful animals in this country, generally a mixture of the Newfoundland and Saint Bernard species, and many incidents are told of their faithful services.

Long before noon we reached Peregoy's, a mountain hotel, twelve or fifteen miles from its nearest neighbor. This was built on a small spot sufficiently destitute of timber to allow the sunlight to enter. It is an excellent place to stop, though so

GENERAL VIEW OF YOSEMITE VALLEY.

far from any settlement. This house stood nearly six thousand feet above the level of the sea, and here ice forms nearly every night in the year. We lunched and rested a while, and then pressed on.

The approach to Yosemite Valley is such that a person would never imagine that just before him is one of the greatest curiosities in the world. In some places you ascend to the very edge of the chasm, where the wall is four thousand feet perpendicular, and almost before you are aware of it you look into the fearful depths beneath. The first view of the valley is ordinarily from Inspiration Point. This name is not given because of any additional beauty that is seen here which is not found at almost every point of the valley, but from the effect felt by the suddenness of the scene that bursts upon the view.

Whatever may have been the freaks of your imagination before you arrive, whatever may have been the description given of the contour of this scene, you find all has been a failure in conveying an idea of this wonder that now charms you, and yet, at the same time, awes you into silence. It may be said, without exaggeration, of many tourists, as they have stood for the first time upon the brink of this chasm,—

> "They spake not a word;
> But, like dumb statues or breathless stones,
> Stared on each other, and looked deadly pale."

One of our own party, a gentleman, too, of fair nerve-power, when he stood looking into the valley below, became agitated and was compelled to withdraw and lie down and rest till his nerves became calm and he somewhat accustomed to the view.

It is easy to conceive that a person could look *downward* a mile or more without any very unpleasant feelings. But let that view downward be associated with dizzy heights upward, and the sensation is wholly different. Here is an incomparable fissure with perpendicular walls of four thousand feet and more in places. In these walls are rugged indentures that are plainly visible, even for miles, in the clear mountain air. Yonder are huge bowlders, weighing thousands upon thousands of tons, piled as if by the hands of Hercules, flung, no doubt, in the unknown centuries past from these heights around us. And about these, or farther out in the valley, as if to escape fearful associations, are great, stalwart trees, two, three hundred feet in height, that look like dwarfs. And trees cling to the rugged sides, here and there, as if held by unknown hands. And the Merced River, like a silver ribbon glistening in the sunlight, runs through all this wild spectacle, as if in sheer contrast to give additional awe.

Then there, on the very verge of the wall, stand Sentinel Rocks, like stony warriors that they are, watching carefully the ages as they pass. Above these still tower higher rocky peaks, holding eternal snows, or bearing the misty burdens of the clouds. While around you is the deep forest, whose branches make mournful music in the wind, —such music, taken in its association with these scenes, as the world does not repeat. Well may it be said,—

"A wondrous scene of nature is displayed."

That the reader may have a correct idea of the topography of the place, it may be stated that the valley lies nearly east and west. Its main axis runs a little north of east by a little south of west. It may be considered as possessing three distinct parts,—the surrounding wall of solid rock, varying in height from one thousand to six thousand feet; the slope of rocky masses and fragments which have fallen from the face of the cliffs, forming a sort of talus or escarpment along the foot of this wall from seventy-five to three hundred and fifty feet high; and then the nearly level bottom-land lying between these slopes, forming the valley proper, and divided into two equal parts by the Merced River flowing through westerly from end to end.

The whole valley is from five to seven miles in length, the bottom of which is four thousand feet above the level of the sea. The rocky wall which shuts it in will average fully three-quarters of a mile in height.

Yosemite Fall is the most prominent object that meets the eye, unless it be some of the bald, rocky peaks that mount to the very clouds. This fall belongs to Yosemite Creek, which has its rise among the melting snows on the mountains above the valley. This fall has a descent of more than two thousand six hundred feet, and is, as far as known, the greatest fall in the world. It is sixteen times higher than Niagara. The entire descent is made in three leaps. The water strikes a projecting ledge after an uninterrupted fall of sixteen hundred feet. Then there is a series of beautiful cascades for six hundred feet, when the final majestic plunge is taken of more than four hundred feet more.

Bridal Veil Creek has its rise on the south side of the valley, and pours into the valley over the face of Cathedral Rock, nine hundred feet, into the depths beneath. Here it forms one of the finest views ever beheld by mortal eyes. The water when it makes its leap over the precipice seems to retain its identity no longer; it is etherealized and, we might almost add, glorified. The action of the wind separates the particles until they are not so much as water in its ordinary form, nor is it spray, but a spiritualized mist that seems too soft, too delicate, to be influenced by gravitation, but that it should be ascending towards the upper realms. The wind toys with it like a ribbon of silk or a veil of gauze, and the lines come into the mind,—

> "Who could wear a veil like this?
> No sooner asked than answered,—
> Why, Maid o' the mist."

Of all the objects in Yosemite Valley, there is nothing so unique as Bridal Veil Fall. Yosemite Falls are greater in their leap, the Vernal grander, and the Nevada more majestic, because a much greater body of water; but for unequalled delicateness and a beauty that charms, Bridal Veil stands without a rival.

The greatest falls in the valley are the Nevada and Vernal,—greatest, because of the amount of water carried over them. They are both on the Merced River, and were it not for the two great descents called by the names of these falls, it might probably be said that there is but one fall. For the Merced River descends more than two thousand feet in less than two miles. Seven hundred feet are taken out of this for the Nevada Fall, and three hundred and fifty for the Vernal Fall, and the rest, a thousand feet and more, for a series of charming cascades, that would be taken for real falls, were it not that they are surpassed by the incomparable grandeur of the great falls above and below them.

Mirror Lake lies nearly opposite from Glazier Point and Sentinel Dome, seemingly, and yet it is really a good distance up the valley, right under the eternal guardianship of North and South Domes; it lies just between the two. But you seem to be fairly opposite nearly everything in this valley. The contour of mountain and valley is such, and the clear, pure air brings out the outlines so distinctly, that you seem to be in full view and near by every object. Mirror Lake is one of the unique sights of the Pacific Coast. If Bridal Veil charms, and Yosemite and Nevada Falls awe you, Mirror Lake will enrapture you. It is like looking into a sea glass, and that mingled with fire when the rays of the sun fall aslant it. Looking at it you are reminded of John's declaration in Revelation : " And before the throne there was a sea of glass like unto crystal. . . . And I saw as it were a sea of glass mingled with fire: and them that had gotten the victory over the beast, and over his image, and over his mark, and over the number of his name, stand on the sea of glass."

A nearer view changes the scene, but not the interest. You seem to be looking almost into ether, so clear, so pure is the water. The grand old mountains look down upon you with such an awfulness as never came from mountain before, you think; while there they are just as plainly looking up from everlasting depths beneath. If a photo-

EL CAPITAN—YOSEMITE.

graph were taken of some object on the shore it would show quite as distinctly in the water as above it.

And the trees, as they stand around, are reflected just as plainly from the water as the tree appears itself. Like Tahoe, it reveals many of its mysteries that lie water-cased, but not concealed, in the regions below,—it is so nearly transparent.

I have no doubt but the position of this lake adds very greatly to its charms. On the north of it is North Dome, an exceedingly high point, and dome-shaped. South or Half Dome is on the other side of the lake, and is the only object of the entire valley that is always present. Go where you will, there is this monarch looking down upon you. It is the highest point in the walls of the valley; higher than El Capitan by nearly eight hundred feet. No human foot has ever trodden the summit, and perhaps never will. Half of this dome has gone, cut from summit to base as smoothly as if by some instrument. It has been a source of a good deal of discussion as to where the other half of this dome has gone, and how it was cleaved asunder. Between these two conical mountains is a considerable forest of those stately pine-trees that add to the beauty of the valley, and that fringe the walls around. Hood's beautiful lines are suggested by the trees that skirt the valley:

> "The pines,—those old gigantic pines
>   That writhe, recalling soon
> The famous human group that writhes
>   With snakes in wild festoon,—
> In famous wrestlings interlaced,
>   A forest Laocoon,—
> Like Titans of primeval girth
>   By tortures overcome,
> Their brown, enormous limbs they twine,
>   Bedewed with tears of gum."

The question has often arisen in the minds of the curious, What made Yosemite Valley? It is without a rival. Lakes are found on this coast that seem to have sunken away hundreds of feet beneath the surface, and are surrounded by perpendicular walls, but nothing like Yosemite. Here, it seems, the regions beneath gave way and let this entire valley, an area of from seven to ten square miles, sink perpendicularly down for nearly four thousand feet. There is a theory advanced that the bottom, by some unknown cause, gave way. Another is, that by volcanic action in some unknown age in the past these mountains were thrown up, leaving the valley as it is. The first theory is certainly the more reasonable, for the physical appearance of walls and summits would not indicate an upheaval of the mountains, but a sinking down of the valley. Whatever it is, the Infinite One alone knows the secret. He leaves it here, sublime, awe-inspiring, as it is, in the midst of these everlasting mountains, an ever-enduring evidence of His greatness and power; bearing not in blazoned letters, such as mortals make, but in silent language, that God reveals, the truth here so plainly taught, and that all hearts should recognize —" The Lord God omnipotent reigneth."

CHAPTER XV.

INTERESTING PLACES AND THINGS.

> " Nature herself, it seemed, would raise
> A minster to her Maker's praise!
> Not for a meaner use ascend
> Her columns, or her arches bend."—SCOTT.

By overland you enter California in the early morning. And almost suddenly, if it be winter or spring, is the transition from snow and cold blasts to flowers and green fields. One will never forget the emotions that are stirred under such change and scenes.

Perhaps the most varied scenery in the world is to be found on the Pacific Coast. Nature seems to have made this in a sense the world's museum. What can be found as the strange products of almost all other countries are here as the heritage of one State. Wonderful agricultural products, the most awe-inspiring scenery, dizzy heights, and dizzier depths,—some of these meet the traveller everywhere.

To the observant tourist, if he have a spirit that readily catches the beautiful, in however rugged a garb it may come, even the rough jogging of the stage-travel furnishes him an experience more enchanting than the most fascinating novel.

An ocean of golden grain, or a vast expanse of purest green, gorgeously bespangled with a thousand flowers, or, perchance, something wholly different,—a rugged cañon, so weird-like and yet so grand withal, that the most lurid anticipations have never even completed a respectable ghostly outline of the scene, stretches away on every side.

> "On the mountains is freedom! the breath of decay
> Never sullies the fresh flowing air;
> Oh! Nature is perfect wherever we stray;
> 'Tis man that deforms it with care."

Staging is a popular mode of locomotion in the West. It is not the most convenient nor the most comfortable, but it is highly novel, and gives ample time for minute observations, and never fails to furnish something amusing, or often ridiculous.

Upon one of these routes running out of the beautiful city of Sacramento there was a singular yet interesting quartet. A Chinaman held the outside, while two gentlemen, merchants of Sacramento, and a clergyman of one of the leading denominations of America,—a very noted man, by the way,—occupied the inside of the stage. The latter gentleman was of excessive corpulency, whose avoirdupois measured well up towards three hundred. On the way a severe storm arose. The clergyman being a very humane gentleman opened negotiations with his travelling companions to allow the Chinaman a place inside out of the rain. The clergyman and one of the merchants took the back seat, while the other and the Mongolian took the other seat, bringing the knees of the Chinaman and clergyman together. After knocking together a spell the minister, measuring across the Chinaman's knees and trying to imitate his vernacular, said, "Too muchee knees, John, too muchee knees." The Chinaman felt the admonition, but opened his unfathomable almond eyes and surveyed for a moment the tremendous amount of human fat that was crowding him, and laconically remarked, at the same time drawing his hand, like a butcher's knife, across the minister's stomach, "Too muchee belly, Mellicanman, too muchee belly; cut him in two, *twice*." The reply was so apropos and witty that all three gentlemen after that were the close friends of the Chinaman.

The route from San Francisco, for that seems to be the starting-point to almost all points on the

Pacific Coast, to the world-renowned Geysers, is one of the most delightful.

Outside of Iceland, these are the only geysers of any magnitude yet discovered, and by far the greatest yet seen. Hot springs can frequently be found, but hot springs are not geysers. But a few miles from where I write hot springs send their heated breath as from the pipes of many steamboats,—thus giving the name "steamboat springs,"—while the water in the coldest snowy day bubbles and hisses with intense heat. But these are geysers only in the most insignificant sense.

Sonoma County, north of San Francisco a distance of about sixty miles, has the distinction of being the location of curiosities that have not been, and perhaps never will be, duplicated in the world's history.

The emotion must be experienced—it can never be described—of going to these weird, Tartarean fields. How awful, how strange, the effect! It stirs up an emotion that is rarely felt.

A lawyer in San Francisco once pointed to a will lying on his table, and said to me, "A young man visited the Geysers and was so impressed with the awfulness of the scene that he was induced to make that will,—they forcibly impressed upon him the brevity of life."

Such would be the effect upon very few minds. But no one having the feeling of a human being can stand amid these boiling, roaring cauldrons, and walk this quaking ground, and smell these fumes, and see these sights, and not feel that an arm invisible and infinite sustains all these things.

The view of the Geysers from the hotel is a very striking one, more especially in the morning, when the steam can be plainly seen issuing from the earth in a hundred different places, the numerous columns uniting at some distance above the earth and forming an immense cloud, which overhangs the rugged cañon.

As the sun advances above the hills this cloud is speedily "eaten up," and the different columns of steam, with the exception of those from the Steamboat Geyser, the Witches' Cauldron, and a few of the more noted, become invisible at a short distance, being evaporated as fast as they issue from the ground.

The unearthly-looking cañon, in which most of the springs are situated, makes up into the mountains directly from the river. A small stream of water, which rises at the head of the cañon, flows through the whole length. The stream is pure and cold at its source, but gradually becomes heated, and its purity greatly marred as the waters of the various springs flow into it.

Hot springs in close proximity to cold springs, white, red, and black sulphur springs, iron, soda, and boiling alum springs, all pour their strangely medicated waters into this little stream, until its once pure and limpid water, like a human patient made sick by over-dosing, becomes pale, and has a wheyish, sickly, unnatural look, as it feverishly tosses and tumbles over its rocky bed.

A short distance up this cañon a deep, dark pool is seen, which is the receptacle of the waters of all the springs above it. By the time the conglomerate waters reach this pool they are greatly cooled in temperature, and the basin, it is said by some, forms a delightful bath. Our ideas of baths were not met here, however, and we did not indulge. A few feet from this there is a warm alum and iron spring, whose waters are very strongly impregnated.

Farther up the cañon the springs become very numerous, and boil and bubble everywhere. The water in the stream that came down the cañon is very hot. One is hardly contented to move lest the seemingly treacherous ground should give way, or he be precipitated into a boiling cauldron.

Magnesia, alum, tartaric acid, Epsom salts, or some other medicine, can be picked up very frequently.

Strange sounds greet the ear, some hissing like water on a hot iron, or softly purring or whistling, or a loud roaring sound. One has a sound like the machinery of a grist-mill, hence it is called the "Devil's Grist-mill."

High above all the sounds is the roaring of the Steamboat Geyser. The steam from this geyser issues with very great force from a hole perhaps two feet in diameter. It is heated to such a temperature that it is nearly invisible until it rises some distance from the ground. It is ordinarily dangerous to approach near it.

One of these geysers throws up water as black as ink, and strange, it is in close proximity to water that is quite clear. Others that are boiling hot are but a very few feet from those that are "ice cold." The varied sounds that run through all the gamut are mingled with the deep subterranean roar similar to that which precedes an earthquake.

The impressions made upon the memory by these scenes and sounds will never be obliterated. Time grows old, but they last. These objects of so rare a character remain to impress the tens of thousands that shall yet visit them.

> "They do not die,
> Nor change to us, although they change."

Above this county, to the northward, is the county of Mendocino, noted for its celebrated dairies and rugged coast scenes. Very queer formations are seen in the rocky cliffs that overhang the sea. The waves have washed great holes, leaving caves that reach some distance back under the overhanging rocks.

These milch ranches have become noted over the entire land as among the greatest and best in the world. Mendocino butter brings the best price in the home markets, and it finds a ready sale in foreign countries, to which large quantities are shipped. Hundreds of cows are milked upon one ranch, and thousands upon thousands in the county.

There is no place in California where tourists can spend a month more pleasantly enjoying the natural scenery, the hospitality of the farmers, and the exhilarating climate, than in Mendocino County.

CHAPTER XVI.

A GLIMPSE AT THE "HEATHEN CHINEE."

"For ways that are dark and for tricks that are vain,
The heathen Chinee is peculiar."—BRET HARTE.

WE always did think the above couplet a rattling kind of ditty; but, notwithstanding that, it contains a fair average of truth. For the "dark ways" and "vain tricks" and *peculiarity* of this people, or of such as reach these shores, are very striking, to say nothing of the pure, heathenish practices of these Orientals,—for heathens they are of the most absolute type.

It would terribly harrow up the moral sensibilities of many were they told that heathenism, with its pernicious influences, was strongly established upon these Christian shores.

Many can read of it as a fixture, natural, and as a matter of course, in the Oriental Empire, without much distress of soul, because distance may measurably relax the tension of the religious sensibilities, but gasp a prayer for legal barriers against its encroachments upon the land of Christian freedom.

Some, never having had an opportunity to investigate its magnitude or its nefarious influences, are readily inclined to look upon it in the Golden State as a mere immoral pigmy that will vanish before the power of Christianity. Both of these classes may be partially mistaken; it has a stronger foothold than the first would suppose, and does not vanish half so readily as the other would think.

Few persons have a proper conception of it as it is, because, first, existing among an entirely different nationality from our own, they have not marked its influences, and then, like many evils around us everywhere, it is measurably disregarded.

While many things in connection with the Chinese immigration to this coast is to be deprecated, it is not such a moral stench, or political incubus, or social want that some politicians would have us believe. The great danger is not, as some assert, in the very presence of the Orientals, but in the possibility of them coming in such numbers as to entirely overrun, Goth- and Vandal-like, the entire coast. Their moral ideas are low,—nobody doubts that; their prejudice against our institutions and customs is very strong. Their religious tenets, if we may so speak, are directly antagonistic to all our ideas of Christianity and religion. But these must not be used as a weapon against this individual nationality. For other comers to these shores have low moral ideas, too, and are prejudiced as much against our republican institutions, and have religious views which are certainly but little, if any, better, while they are far more *Jesuitical* in their operations than all Chinadom put together. *And yet they are citizens.*

This is not written in defence of any of the bad features of the Chinese,—nor any of the good ones either, for that matter,—but rather, before writing further, to indicate that there may be an irrational prejudice against this people.

Once, during a few weeks' stay in San Francisco, I made it one of my efforts to see what I could of heathenism as it is practised by the Chinese in that city. No one has fully seen San Francisco who has not gone through and closely observed its heathen quarter.

We rather like the idea of running away to Europe to see the sights before seeing one's own country; it indicates brilliancy (?). Certainly tourists should see the wonders of our own land,—wonders beyond conception; wonders in the mountains and in the valleys,—there the impress of the Divine hand is plainly seen. Go into this gorgeous city of opulence if you would see the highest adornments of art and the superlative evidences of licentious minds. But for examples of moral depravity and the degradation to which beings calling themselves human can, yea, do, reach, but sweep along the low, dingy corridors and the small, filthy apartments—too filthy to be called rooms—of the heathen part of this great city. You learn more in one day's investigation of humanity's degradation and depravity than in a lifetime of theorizing.

Some one has, I believe, written up "New York by Gaslight," because its iniquities can better be seen after nightfall. So with Chinese life; if you would see them *as they are*, look at them in the sickly light of their tallow candles, and the feeble, flickering, accursed glare of their opium-lamps. Thus only can a proper view behind the scenes be had.

With the necessary police-guides we made a tolerably fair inspection of that Sodom part of the city. I say with the necessary police-guides, because however carelessly you may walk through Chinatown in daylight, your life might go at a cheap rate after night.

These ignorant people, I am informed, are quiet and submissive so long as they remain in the minority, but are dangerous and revengeful when in the majority. Hence the danger after the day's labors are past, when they are all congregated in their hovels, game-houses, shops, etc.

The emotional powers of the Chinese seem to be under extraordinary control, or measurably extinct, for wherever you see these sons of the Orient you see the same non-demonstrative people, whether on the railroad, the busy street, or in their miserable quarters; and the most exciting game or pleasing play can do little more than call forth a puff of opium-smoke. The most imperfect sanitary system—if system it may be called at all—is practised by this people. No cleanliness and no pure air grace their rooms or greet their olfactories. And how ordinary health can be enjoyed by them is a marvel to all.

Our police-guide led us through narrow alleys, and gloomy, miserable cellars in which would be literally piled away from fifteen to twenty-five Chinamen, with no sign of beds but rude pieces of slabs. Upon these they lounge and smoke their opium from their queer club-pipes till they gradually sink to the floor and are asleep. Think of a lifetime spent in this way! Hardly a comfort, and not a single luxury. No downy beds, sociables, or tables, or even chairs, to think not of flowers, paintings, or music! The cooking for all the inmates of some of the rooms, each doing his own, is done upon one little fire, made, perchance, in the corner on a stone. Many of these hovels had no floors, and many of them were covered with mud and water.

"Are these persons not very sickly?" we asked our guide:

"Seldom sick; very few of them had the smallpox when that disease was bad in the city," he replied.

"What do these fellows do for a living?" we asked.

"Steal," was the brief answer.

I suppose it was so, for a more degraded and vicious-looking set of men I never expect to see. Had not our policeman been armed to the teeth, uncomfortable sensations might have been experienced by us all.

We were first led through their noted gambling-house to their theatre. As we passed through, the policeman in advance, one of our party dropped behind, when suddenly a burly old Chinaman seized him, and had it not been for prompt interference the consequences might have been bad.

This people have more activity of intellect than they ordinarily get credit for. Those of them that do business at all make it quite lucrative. Some of them have become very wealthy. There are none of them but can demand their money for the least service rendered with as much *nonchalance* as the most experienced speculator. But when you consider their moral sensibilities,—ah, there's the rub. This department of the mental mechanism is certainly very much dwarfed. A home in America, even for a number of years, seems to have very little effect upon their spiritual natures. What effect is being made down deep in their hearts by their contact with the American people of course cannot be told, but to all appearances the effect is but slight. Missionaries are laboring faithfully and with some success, but a success that seems very meagre.

The *feeding* of the dead bodies of their departed friends—a heathen practice—is followed here as tirelessly as in the Orient itself. And among the better class, when not enjoying even the common comforts of life, can be found many little deities to which they regularly pay homage, while many of the worse class seem not even to have so much as this kind of devotion, yet I suppose they have.

This people in their own land must have a low standard of morals. There is certainly but little in their social life or religious dogmas to greatly elevate their standard of moral freedom. But, notwithstanding this, we are inclined to think that their morals are lower here than at home. The motive that brings them here—a sordid one—does not, to say the least, augment their ideas and practices of right.

Then, here they are virtually without the influence of female society. True, woman in China is far below her real standard, and is not looked upon with her refining power as she is here; but however low she may be, however little her true power and worth are valued, she, in a refining sense, must be more beneficial than the presence of no woman at all. We doubt if humanity ever gets so low that sister, wife, and mother cease to have an influence.

There are a few Chinese women on this coast, but the most of them are of the basest kind. A few of the merchants have brought their families, but if they are of the aristocracy their wives and daughters are seldom seen, except upon rare occasions.

There is one practice—of which we were informed by our intelligent policeman—that not only illustrates the depravity of this people, but certainly calls for the most positive condemnation of all lovers of law and morality. I refer to buying and selling of Chinese females,—literally, the farming-out of women. A female—an outcast, of course—is brought from China and farmed out to the highest bidder, who in turn makes merchandise of her, the woman having no more control over her moral or even physical condition, often, than the caged animals of Woodward's Gardens.

Of course these transactions are carried on in comparative secrecy. Yet we were assured that they were known to exist, and that, too, by the authorities. Nor can these things be easily avoided, though in a Christian city, where there are thousands crowded together in a comparatively small area, and that, too, where manners and language are of an entirely different nationality.

We cannot but in our inmost heart pity this deluded people, that have but few comforts, no luxuries, to our way of thinking, and withal no standard of morals.

We had now seen the lowest features of what we may call the physical existence of China-life in this country. But there was still another feature that we had not seen, and that was their worship—their temples. Two we visited were fitted up for the masses, and one seemed to be especially for the wealthy part of the population.

A very intelligent young man, a Christian, offered to go with us to the temples, and there explain the various parts of the heathen worship. There was great similarity in many of the features of the three Joss-houses we visited. They manifested very little taste in the external appearance of these temples, as they looked like other common, dingy houses. The interior is generally decorated very gorgeously, and, of course, stuffed with gods

"Of such frightful mien," etc.

As we entered the first temple there, in the presence of the sanctity (?) of these grim deities, we were accosted by an old fortune-teller, who had his cards, money, etc., spread out before him. A number of dirty little urchins whistled and jumped irreverently before the altars.

"Sit down here, and we will see them worship," said our Oriental friend, as two young men entered bearing a heavily-laden basket. They prostrated themselves in pure Eastern style before the deities; then, after much bowing, they spread before the gods a cooked chicken, cakes, and wine. A huge wooden tiger by the door had its decaying jaws filled with spoiled meat. This was pure heathen worship, but, nevertheless, it seemed to be very devout.

How true that man is a worshipping being! As naturally as the needle turns to the pole will man's affections centre somewhere. How essential that the real object be not a god but GOD!

CHAPTER XVII.

"HARD LINES" IN TRAVEL.

"Ay, now am I in Arden; the more fool I; when I was at home I was in a better place; but travellers must be content."— SHAKSPEARE.

DID you ever make a trip to Arizona? I did; and for genuine hard times and rough living it was about equal to Kane's trip to the North Pole, excepting the fact that I returned alive.

It happened thus. Once, in conversation with a friend in San Francisco, the proposition came up to go to some new country. He proposed Arizona, and as that was likely to "fill the bill" for novelty, we were agreed at once.

Tickets were purchased on the steamer "Senator" for Wilmington, the "embarcadero" of Los Angeles. As economy was the order of the day, we secured steerage passage, my friend remarking "that we would save fifteen dollars each, and as the trip was only forty hours, we could not make money easier." How easy it is for one to be mistaken we soon found out.

We steamed out of the bay Sabbath morning, and as we remained on deck to see all the sights, we did not realize being steerage passengers until the bell rang for dinner. It was then time to look out for the "main chance."

On the lower deck we found suspended a wide plank, perhaps twenty feet long, which served for a table; and as it was fully five feet from the deck, chairs or stools would have been of little use, even if the company had not forgotten to furnish them.

The standing room would have been good, but for the fact that some enterprising genius was transporting thirty or forty mules to the lower country, and they were ranged each side of the "table," in good fair kicking distance of the unfortunate crowd of hungry men.

Fortunately the boiled beef, poor potatoes, and "hard tack" did not so fully occupy our attention but that we had time to dodge the heels of some unusually lively mule.

We had our blankets, and a wagon-body on deck furnished us a fair resting-place. The forty hours were a constant repetition, and we earned our fifteen dollars.

Just here let me say, always travel first-class, or else stay at home, for first-class is poor enough for any one.

In due time Wilmington was reached, or rather the steamer's anchorage, for she did not go nearer than six or seven miles of the landing. We were taken ashore by a small steamboat, huddled together like a flock of sheep, and at last we of the steerage were on an equal footing with those of the cabin.

Thirty miles staging over a level plain brought us to Los Angeles, then, as now, a modern paradise. Economy still prevailing, we hunted a fourth-class hotel, and found it. The thermometer showing 108° in the shade, we thick-blooded San Franciscans thought it the hottest place on earth, but we found out our mistake before reaching the Colorado.

Upon making inquiries as to the best way to get to Arizona, we soon found it was a "terra incognita" to almost every one. My friend now weakened on the trip, and went to work at his trade, but as I had started, I proposed to go through. I found among the passengers a man of the same mind, who said "he should see the Colorado or die trying." So we joined hands and purses, bought three horses, packed one with an enormous load, comprising all the useless articles we could think of, and rode the other two. With an early start, and continued hard work in revising our pack animal, during which we discovered we were not proficient packers, by ten o'clock at night we reached Mud Springs, on the road to San Bernardino twenty-eight miles.

The next morning we found that owing to the pack having lost its equilibrium so many times during the previous day, our horse needed "re-constructing," or some other form of renovating. My partner and self agreed that packing was poor business, and we had enough of it. So we traded one horse, saddle, and bridle, and one hundred and twenty dollars in coin, for an old red Concord buggy, worth perhaps twenty-five dollars, if a man wanted it and was determined to have it. That poor buggy, how well I remember it! I do not think it was in the ark, but it was nearly old enough. We then hitched in our two unbroken "mustangs," and away we went, working our passage all the time. We arrived, at the end of the second day, with a broken buggy and half-broken team, at San Bernardino, distant from Los Angeles sixty-four miles.

Here we found a valley that gave the promise (now fulfilled) of being one of the most beautiful on earth.

We stayed here two weeks to refit and recruit ourselves and stock; also bought another worthless horse, and enough trash to freight a camel. When we had no excuse for longer delay, we put everything we possibly could on our pack-horse, and the balance in the wagon. Of course one of us had to walk, and as our new purchase had a will of his own, and would not lead behind our "coach," the "walkist" must drag the obstinate brute.

We started at five in the morning.we hardly

knew for where, and a harder day's work I hope never to have before me, the thermometer, which we always carried, showing 115° in the shade, and no one will ever know how high in the sun. At nine o'clock at night, when nearly used up, we saw a light in the distance, and struck a bee-line for it, as it had been too dark for some time to follow a road or trail. We were soon warned that we were approaching a human habitation by the fierce barking of something less than twenty dogs, great and small. We soon reached the open door of a large "adobe" farm-house, from which the light we had followed shone,—a very beacon to the traveller. In the doorway appeared the cheery face of the lady of the house, and behind her were ranged children from the young lady to the small infant on the floor.

We found here a resting-place hard to beat in any country. Here, on the very summit of the "Sierras," was a family consisting of a man and wife and ten children. On this self-same spot had they passed their days since '50, as it were on the very edge of the universe, for the great desert never counts in speaking of the inhabitable earth. Each member of the family appeared to vie with the others in doing the most for our comfort, and we were surfeited with grapes, and such grapes! water- and musk-melons, peaches, figs, almonds, etc., etc., grown on their own place, until we began to feel that it would be a good thing to remain the rest of our days. But this life of "dolce far niente" would never get us to Arizona.

According to our usual custom we here made an entire change in our outfit. We exchanged our buggy and horses for a light ambulance and five horses broken to harness. We were also accompanied by one of the boys of the family, some seventeen years of age.

With our wagon filled with provisions, such as "carne seca" or jerked beef, "panola" or ground parched corn, flour, *tobacco*, guns, ammunition, etc., also a spare saddle-horse in case of accident, we made start number three.

The first twenty miles was through the San Gorgonia Pass, a mere gap in the southern extremity of the Sierra Nevada. This pass is about two miles wide, with a gentle descent towards the east, and is a fit portal to the desert waste beyond.

"Agua Blanco" or White Water was reached considerably after dark, and, with a cold bite for supper, we spread our blankets for the night. In the darkness, I spread mine on what appeared like a smooth spot. After all was prepared I lay wearily down, but immediately, without a sign of weariness, I got up without being bid. I had, in my ignorance of the country, selected a bed of the "tuña" or prickly pear, and I do not think I am entirely free from the thorns to this day.

At daylight we were off in style, which style was kept up for at least three hundred yards. Then came an apparently unlimited thicket of "chollas" (pronounced chōyas), and the day was spent in making a road through this very worst species of cactus.

Our camp was made at a spot we named the "Four Palms," from the presence of that number of those beautiful tropical trees. Here we found a spring of splendid-looking water, but appearances were deceitful. It was so strongly impregnated with alkali as to be almost undrinkable. And I may as well say here, that was a sample of all the desert water, some perhaps a little better and some much worse.

The next morning we arose rather stiff and sore from the previous day's labor, but forward was the word; so, taking a hurried breakfast, we took up our line of march. This day we succeeded in getting over twenty-five miles of the worst ground in the universe,—loose white sand, and in places completely undermined by rats till our horses would sink in from one to two feet in depth, making any kind of an advance almost impossible. After dark we came to a spot which we called the "Thousand Palms," because there were too many to count, so we lumped them.

Here let me say parenthetically our thermometer was of no further use, as it was only graduated to

126°, and that would not indicate the temperature in the shade. This spot was a perfect oasis in the surrounding waste. Over a space of about twenty acres were spread the aforesaid thousand palms,— gorgeous in their tropical beauty, reaching to a height of seventy or eighty feet, with their dense tops just fitted to shelter one from the scorching rays of the sun. The ground underneath was covered with an immense growth of grass, sheltering innumerable rattlesnakes, but pleasant nevertheless. This spot, from appearances, very seldom if ever had been trodden by the foot of the white man.

After a splendid night's rest, we took our regular beans and coffee, filled our canteens with water, and started. Travelled all day skirting a thicket of mesquit-bushes, in which thicket in several places could be found plenty of water; but of this we were entirely ignorant, supposing, naturally, we must go to the mountains for water and not in the centre of the sun-parched valley. Our mistake cost us dearly.

At night we camped without water for our animals, and very little for ourselves. And when we started in the morning it was very evident we would not get any great distance with our team. So we were not at all disappointed when, by ten o'clock, our horses stopped and entirely refused to go farther. We unharnessed them and let them go where they pleased. And here we were a greater distance from water, of which we had any knowledge, than we could possibly walk. To understand this fully it is necessary to know that in this dry, hot climate one cannot get along, with any comfort, with less than four gallons of water for twenty-four hours. Without the requisite amount the whole system becomes parched in an incredibly short time.

The points where we supposed we had a certainty of obtaining water was still several miles distant, and as we well knew without it we could neither return nor go on, we pushed ahead.

We took nothing with us except a flask of brandy and a paper of tea, as a person suffering from the want of water never thinks of eating. At dark we had nearly reached a spur of mountain which reached out some considerable distance into the valley.

But as it was impossible to see our way, we lay down upon the sand, and a more woe-begone party was never seen. Death seemed to be in our immediate presence. At the first break of day we were up and moving, though very weak and exhausted.

Upon reaching the spur spoken of above, each took a different ravine and went on a trip of exploration, examining the rocks and ground carefully, and in some places where the sand seemed slightly moist we dug with our tin cups, but without avail. No water to be found.

Near night we came back to the point where we had separated, each reporting failure. The young man with us said he was going to try to get back, and, as his habits of life had fitted him for exercise of that kind, and we had nothing better to offer, we did not attempt to dissuade him from the attempt; so we bade him farewell, and away he went.

My partner and self took another rest on the sand, and in fact did little but talk until the next morning. Then we felt we had no strength for much exertion, but made two or three short trips in the early part of the day with no results.

By nine o'clock we were completely exhausted, and took our station under a small dry weed, to partially shelter our faces from the scorching rays of the midday sun, and prepared to await what might happen. In a short time our tongues became so swollen as to protrude from our mouths, and soon became nearly as black as coal. We thought of our brandy, but we knew well that even a small quantity taken in our present condition would almost instantly destroy reason. But we found it useful to bathe our faces and breathe, reviving us very much.

It would be impossible to describe one's feelings in such a case, but, taken all in all, the absolute suffering was not unbearable. The worst was the continual exertion to retain the senses. If we closed our eyes, at once the most beautiful lakes appeared, surrounded by a fringe of green trees and shrubbery, similar to a mirage.

By noon my partner had almost entirely lost both his reason and power to help himself, and although not able to raise myself, I nearly smothered him with the brandy on his face. Finally I took one of my revolvers, with the intention of killing him and then myself, and ending the misery. But I soon gave up that idea, and threw the pistols as far away as possible to remove the temptation.

At about two o'clock, when hope and reason had nearly left us, we—or rather I, for my partner was past hearing—were thoroughly aroused by a whistle. One moment before I did not think it possible for me to even raise my head, but that single note, indicating the presence of a human being with life enough to make so much noise, did more to restore my vitality and strength than a thousand claps of thunder, and I immediately raised to my elbow. Coming rapidly towards us was an Indian of the Serano tribe, on a horse, and strangely the thought came into my mind that he was the finest specimen of a man I had ever seen, when in reality he was nothing but a fair sample of the dirty, degraded aborigines of that section.

He soon came up with us, and, with a mournful

"pobrecitos" (poor fellows), dismounted from his horse and brought an "olla" or earthen-jar of water. Filling my cup, an ordinary tin one, he put it to my lips, and I suppose I drank it, but I neither felt nor tasted anything. As far as the actual sensation was concerned it was to me a pantomime. But after going through the same motions three or four times I was able to get upon my feet, although a stranger might have supposed I was somewhat intoxicated. We at once went to the assistance of my partner, who was much farther gone than myself. Raising him from the ground, we actually turned cup after cup of the life-preserving liquid down his throat, with as little apparent effect as pouring it into a rat-hole. In the mean time I had taken my share as fast as I could swallow, and felt comparatively well but terribly hungry and weak. Then with our paper of tea we made a dose—I can call it nothing else, it was so strong—which just reached the spot, and answered for food and drink.

In less than an hour the swelling had gone out of our tongues, and they had returned to their normal position. Before two hours had passed we had entirely disposed of five gallons of water and sent the Indian for more. From him we learned that we were only four miles from a well which was out in the valley.

At dark we started under the guidance of our

dusky friend for the well, and upon reaching it felt too happy for utterance.

We explained to him, in Spanish, that we wished to return to our wagon. He evidently understood, but wanted to wait till morning, as he insisted we were too weak to make the trip. We now learned from him that our young friend had accidentally stumbled upon the Indian village, and had the horses brought in, and, as he said, was "all right." Suffice it to say, we joyfully reached the said village by the middle of the next day, and, as our friend had already made a trip to the wagon, which was in full view about two miles distant, and brought in a sack of flour and a few other articles, we at once prepared what was to us one of the most sumptuous meals we ever enjoyed.

The next day we made up our minds it was a bad start, and determined, as soon as we could recruit our stock, to return for a better opportunity. While the recruiting process was going on I spent the time in making myself familiar with the desert, and the knowledge so gained was of great use to me in after-expeditions.

Leaving the wagon and contents in the care of the Indians, with promises of pay if they left it untouched, and threats of death to the whole tribe if we found anything disturbed upon our return, we rode bareback to our starting-point, the "Ranch."

In a few days we did what we should have done at first, bought two good mules, saddles, and bridles, mounted our animals, and went to the Colorado River in five days. So much for ignorance.

CHAPTER XVIII.

INCIDENTS AND OBSERVATIONS IN ARIZONA.

"What! shall this speech be spoke for an excuse,
Or shall we on without apology?"—SHAKSPEARE.

IN a former chapter mention was made of a family living at the extreme verge of civilization, at the entrance to San Gorgonia Pass. This family is worthy of more than a passing notice,—a representative of border life.

The morning after my arrival, soon after daylight, I started out to see what kind of place we had reached. Hearing voices in a large corral back of the house, I went that way for the purpose of finding some one to answer my questions.

But upon reaching the entrance I stopped in sheer surprise. Two of the daughters of the family, girls thirteen and fifteen respectively, were milking. Not the milking, but the manner, was the curiosity. The cows were more than half wild, and one could not go very near them with any safety, even without attempting to milk them. So the elder girl would take an ordinary Mexican "reata," or lasso, and at a distance of thirty or forty feet throw the noose over the horns of a cow; then taking the other end to a post in the centre of the corral, evidently placed there for the purpose, wind it around, thus enabling her to hold the brute, although making desperate exertions to get free.

The younger sister with a whip then urged the animal nearer the post, while the other, by slipping the rope, held all she gained. This was kept up until the cow was finally brought with her head tight to the post, when by putting another rope around the hind legs she could be easily brought to the ground. Then while one held her down by sitting on her head the other did the milking.

Here were two young and beautiful girls performing labor, which very few men in other countries would dare attempt, without any fear or thought that it was at all unusual for young ladies to milk wild cattle.

Some time after I saw these same girls in good society in San Francisco, and no one unacquainted with the fact would imagine for a moment they were not "to the manor born."

The whole family of ten children would compare favorably in the matter of a common school education, manners, or anything that goes to make up the man or woman of to-day, with the residents of any town or city. Nevertheless they were nearly all born and all raised in this self-same spot. They knew and sang all the latest airs, performed passably on several instruments, such as the flute, guitar, violin, etc. Above all, each one of them could write a sensible letter without misspelling half as many words as the average boarding-school graduate.

In going through the San Gorgonia Pass, with the thermometer at 120° in the shade, it is something wonderful to look on either side and see mountains covered in part by eternal snow. The San Jacinto Mountain, on the south, is bluff,—in fact, nearly perpendicular on the side next the desert,—and while its base is washed by the hot waters of the "Agua Caliente" springs, its summit is crowned with everlasting snow. At the mouth of the pass "White Water" breaks from the mountain chain in a volume sufficient to run half a dozen mills, but the sands of the desert absorb it entirely before it runs half a mile.

Many times has the idea been started of using the waters of the Colorado for irrigating the desert through which it runs, both by private individuals and in the halls of Congress, but it is my firm conviction that with the whole volume of that river it would not be possible to reclaim one thousand acres from its natural state of drouth.

At "Martinez," a village of the "Couilla" Indians, about sixty miles from White River, the moisture rises to the surface of the ground every night, and the Indians raise very fair corn, melons, etc., considering the fact that they do not plough or dig more than to cover the seed. Several hundred acres of land here could be brought to a high state of cultivation, and pineapples, bananas, or any tropical fruit could be raised in the greatest perfection. Also at "Dos Palmos" (two palms), twenty-five miles farther on, is a similar spot of perhaps two hundred acres.

To the east of the latter place is the great dry lake, or sea. This lake is in the centre eighty feet below the sea level, and from the facts that for nearly one hundred miles on the south side tide-marks are nearly as plainly visible as on the sea-coast, and that myriads of barnacles still adhere to the rocks, it is evident that the sea covered all this portion of the desert at a not distant time. From observations I am inclined to believe that the old historians who represented Lower California as an island were correct.

There are many stories told of boiling mud-springs and remains of vessels found in this lake-bed, but I have crossed and recrossed it in all directions several times, and have never seen anything of the kind.

But one peculiarity I found. If a spot, greater or smaller, were scraped clean of the loose sand and dirt, within twenty-four hours a bed of pure white salt would form from one-half to two inches in depth.

I am inclined to think an outlay of money not much greater than would be required for the Colorado irrigation scheme would bring the waters of the Gulf of California into their old natural bed, thus giving us an inland sea capable of floating the largest vessels, with a length of one hundred and fifty miles, or even more. This would be the more easily done, as it would be only necessary to cut through the obstruction or accumulation of sand formed in past ages by the gulf itself. And with its rise of tide of thirty-two feet only a small amount of assistance would be required to allow it to force its own channel.

A little distance east of Dos Palmos the trail, at present, turns somewhat to the north, and about a mile from this turn the writer, with a companion, found fourteen dead bodies, nearly all Mexicans, who had evidently perished for want of water, with a fine natural tank within a half-mile containing thousands of gallons.

After turning northeast, in a few miles Cañon Springs are reached. Here is a ravine in itself perfectly dry, but with a number of springs along its banks, more or less impregnated with alkali, for a distance of two miles; but these springs cause no vegetation to put forth, and there is no "blossoming like the rose." This is a good camping-ground; and I once found here about two hundred pounds of the finest bloodstone, which I gathered and stacked up, intending to take it on my return, but some lucky individual forestalled me, and made a neat little sum from my labor.

Some six or seven miles east of Cañon Springs is "Tabaseca," another watering-place, but rather difficult of access. From this point the route lies northeast, across a "mesa" or table-land, for a distance of thirty-five or forty miles, to "Chucawalla," the best watering-place in all that part of the territory. One night in '62, the writer, who, with a party, was camped in the dry ravine at Chucawalla, was aroused at midnight by a roaring like the dash of the waves on the sea-coast, and from former experience knew the sound to be from a waterspout. I immediately awoke my companions in time to save the lives of all, but in scrambling up the bank no time was given to save blankets or saddles, much less provisions, for in one minute the torrent was rushing down to the depth of thirty feet. This only lasted a few moments, and subsided as rapidly as it rose, and by seven in the morning there was no indication that a drop of moisture had ever been seen in that section. Saddles and blankets were gathered up a mile or so below, but we had the pleasure of making the remaining distance to La Paz without provisions of any kind.

The first time my partner and I reached the Colorado was in June, and we found the river ten or eleven miles wide, it having overflowed its banks. As we had very little to eat, and had heard provisions were to be obtained on the other side, we chartered four Mohave Indians to take us across. They soon built a small raft of "tules," and leaving our mules to care for themselves, we went aboard. When we started the top of our float was a foot out of water, with an Indian at each corner for propelling power. By the time the centre of the stream was reached the tules had absorbed so much that we were partially submerged, and when we reached the other side the raft barely supported us, wet as we were to our arm-pits.

Upon landing we found a man from San Diego, with teams and wagons freighted with goods for a store. He built a brush shanty, and opened out in style, on the present site of the town of La Paz.

There is a peculiar style of rattlesnake found in great numbers between Chucawalla and the Colorado bottom worthy of mention. They are small, seldom reaching the length of eighteen inches, with nearly the same color as the sand on which they are found. They have short, horn-like protuberances on the head and neck similar to those of a horned toad. But the great singularity of this reptile is its manner of locomotion, which is by apparently supporting itself by its head and tail; then giving its body a lateral motion, it is carried sidewise a considerable distance, so that it is very uncertain, judging from the way the head is pointing, what course they may take. They are called in the vernacular "sidewollopers," and are extremely poisonous.

Speaking of poisons reminds me. Once I met an old mountaineer, who had been in Arizona. I asked him what kind of a country it was, at the same time telling him I was going there. "Well, young man," said he, "everything that runs, crawls, or flies there, either bites or stings, and the bite or sting is certain death. Every plant, bush, or tree has thorns, and they are all poisonous; and every man is a thief." At that time, fifteen years ago, it was not so far from the truth as some would think.

The first gold discovery in this part of Arizona was made about six miles back from La Paz, in the mountain chain bordering the river. The first placer mining was done by "dry washing,"—a tedious and uncertain way of separating the gold and dirt. This operation is in the first place by winnowing to remove the fine dust, after which, in a round-bottomed iron pan, with a peculiar rotary motion, the gold is settled into the bottom of the pan, and the sand and gravel thrown off. But from the fact that it is a good day's work for one man to wash forty pans per day, the "diggings" must of necessity be rich to pay. The above-mentioned gold-field was called." Camp Ferrar."

For a time copper attracted the attention of miners. Ore was scattered over the whole country of wonderful richness, yielding as high as seventy per cent. copper, and from eighty to one hundred dollars per ton in silver and gold.

Some rich silver deposits were also found in various localities, but no ledges. A great amount of prospecting was done, and a large outlay of capital from Williams's Fork to the mouth of the Gila (pronounced Héla), but nothing that paid was struck till long after.

A party, under the guidance of two old mountaineers, started inland, travelling up Williams's Fork,—a tributary of the Colorado,—and prospected each creek or ravine where there appeared any probability of finding gold. They found nothing worthy of mention until they reached a ravine, with a small stream of water in its bed, on the banks of which was afterward located the town of Weaverville. Here was an abundance of coarse gold, but from the depth of the dirt and gravel in the ravine it was impossible to work to advantage on account of the water filling every hole sunk. Still, with all the disadvantages, a considerable quantity of the precious metal was secured, and a lively camp, with two stores, and whiskey-shops in great profusion, opened out flamingly.

One of the miners had the good fortune to wound a mountain sheep near the town, and it started up the steep side of an adjacent mountain, he following. The chase lasted till the summit was reached, and the sheep eluded his pursuer, who, being weary and almost breathless with the pursuit, seated himself to rest. His eyes happening to rest upon the rock at his feet, he saw something glisten, which upon examination proved to be gold.

He at once went to work, and, with his sheath-knife alone, collected about half a pint of "nuggets" before night. Before the discovery became known to others (five days), he took out sixty pounds, avoirdupois, of very pure coarse gold, worth then seventeen dollars per ounce, troy weight. This was sufficient to give him a trip to Los Angeles, and a fine opportunity for spending it, which he did in about two months, when he returned to look for the next "pocket."

This mountain, from which many thousands of dollars were taken, was a wonder, towering three thousand feet above the surrounding valleys,—a rough but grand mass of granite, looking in the distance like some enormous ruin of past ages. On the tabled summit of this pile, loosely distributed in the seams and fissures, and scarcely covered with any soil or dirt, were found large quantities of gold, mostly in the form of lumps and worn "chispas."

I "dry-washed" one winter on this mountain, in company with three others, and we took out about five dollars per day to the man, but, as it cost six to live, we did not accumulate great wealth. We furnished our own pack animal and keg to bring us water from the valley below, and paid twenty-five cents per gallon beside. We lived five days on boiled beans "straight," that is, with nothing else, not even salt. Afterwards we paid six dollars for a three-pound sack of this necessary seasoning, after which the bill of fare was improved.

The price of all articles of food, without regard to the first cost, was one dollar and a half per pound. Beans, potatoes, coffee, flour, sugar, bacon, etc., all the same.

I "washed" faithfully one week, from Monday morning till Saturday noon, without a "color," and Saturday afternoon took out one hundred and fifty dollars. That was my last work on the mountain. I concluded to leave while I had money enough.

An incident occurred here that cannot be accounted for by any ordinary human hypothesis. A party of us were going on a prospecting expedition to the "Hassyampa," a cañon eighteen miles from Weaverville. An honest Dutchman asked permission to make one of the party, to which we consented. He packed his only horse and started on, expecting us to soon overtake him, as we were all mounted.

His directions were to take the left-hand fork of the trail two miles from town. We started after a time and rode pretty fast to overtake our friend, as the country was filled with Apache Indians, the worst of all tribes. We passed the fork of the trail without thought, but soon the question arose, Where has the man gone? No tracks of horse or man were to be seen, and as we had no time to spare, we tried to think he had gone back, although we really feared the Apaches had found and murdered him. We went on and camped at the head of the cañon, which was a rugged gorge, twenty miles long. The next day we kept together in our prospecting for safety, and about three o'clock in the afternoon here came our Dutchman. Of course, we were as much surprised as if he had risen from the dead, and questions poured forth in torrents. In a cold, phlegmatic way, he told us that he took the *right*-hand trail, as we had told him, and got into the lower end of the cañon about dark. Here he found a good fire and some "mescal" (century plant) cooking, and thought it was a good place to camp, so picketed his horse and stayed all night. In the morning he cooked and ate his breakfast, packed up, and walked through the whole length of this gap in the mountain range. The wonder of all this was, that at least three hundred of the very worst tribe of Apaches were known to be in the mouth of this cañon, and he had evidently taken possession of one of their camp fires, when five hundred well-armed men could not have followed his track with any degree of safety. The explanation is about this: It is known that the Indians are very fearful of an insane person, thinking that the devil has possession of him; and they, evidently, seeing this man alone walking right into their midst, thought he was insane and abandoned the field to him.

The Territory of Arizona, so long unknown and unexplored, is being settled very rapidly, and the next five years, with the assistance of railroads, will undoubtedly develop its wonderful mineral wealth to a great degree. Without its *metallic richness* it would be as well if it remained a "*terra incognita*" till the end of time. The extreme barrenness of a great portion of its surface will forever forbid its standing prominent in agriculture. But in my opinion no country can excel it as a gold and silver producer, not to mention lead, copper, iron, and nearly every known mineral or metal, when once easy transportation is secured.

With the exception of the sections bordering on the Colorado and Gila Rivers, and the extreme eastern portion, this has long been the home of the

Apache, and very few cared to dispute the title. The Colorado bottom is held by the Mojaves and Yumas, but the white man has begun his work of extermination, and in a few years from now they will surely become extinct. On the Gila are the villages of the Maricopa and Pima Indians, tribes more than half civilized, who devote their time to stock and grain raising. During the time of the existence of the overland stage these people furnished a great portion of the feed for the stations, as well as large quantities of provisions. Upon the taking off of the stage-line they, supposing they were driven off by the Apaches, made a proposition "that if it was started again they would put on three thousand warriors to protect it." The loss of a market was a great disappointment to them.

In various portions of the territory are found evidences of a very remote occupation of the country by some more than half-civilized race. On Salt River the writer saw a small valley, which had evidently been under cultivation, as there was still a "zanja" or ditch, only partially filled up, that had been large enough to carry all the water of the river, which would be sufficient to irrigate the whole valley. There was also an enclosure of rough granite rocks, about six feet high, divided into forty rooms, of an average of ten feet square, undoubtedly intended as a place of refuge from attacks of Indians.

Scattered around this fort were small rectangular ridges, which were without doubt the remains of "adobe" houses. From the number of these ruins there must have been a population of five or six hundred. On an adjacent hill was a small lookout fort of great solidity, probably used as an observatory, with the view of warning the inhabitants of the valley of the approach of danger.

Salt River is a stream of slightly brackish water, that where it exists at all is about twenty-five yards wide by a depth of ten or twelve feet. It may run this size one mile or ten, and then disappears suddenly, to reappear as suddenly after a space greater or less, according to the locality.

There are a great many other places of similar character scattered over the country, some showing signs of great antiquity, of which the Painted Rocks are an instance. These rocks are covered with pictures of animals and men, and also unknown characters or hieroglyphics, which are cut or engraved in the solid stone. Many of these animals, such as the buffalo, grizzly bear, etc., are not, and, as far as we know, never have been, natives of that part of this continent; and, as far as I can ascertain, no one has been able to decipher the characters.

Above Tucson, in the vicinity of "Pino Alto," are the Mowry and Colt mines. The latter of these was discovered eighteen or twenty years ago by a German named Heintzelman, after whom the mine was named. In '62 it was sold to Colonel Colt, of revolver fame, who at once made arrangements to go to work on a large scale. Under the management of Professor Ehrenberg a mill was erected, and sufficient work done to prove this to be one of the richest deposits, if not the richest, in the world. But the Apaches killed off the employees, Ehrenberg alone escaping, and destroyed the works as far as they were able. Since then nothing has been done either in that or the Mowry.

Nothing but a railroad can make this section tenable for the white man. Only the excitement of the search for gold and silver could have caused the rapid development of the last ten years. The immigration came both from the east and west. On the west, to the Colorado, and founded the towns of La Paz, Callville, and Hardyville. On the east, the objective point was the old military station of Tucson (pronounced too-sone), on the Gila River.

As mentioned in a previous chapter, the western portion of Arizona did not prove of much value, as no defined ledges of much worth were ever discovered. Some deposits of considerable richness were found, but they were not sufficiently large to warrant the outlay of much capital, consequently very little has been done towards opening up this section.

As a matter of fact, considerable mining, both in "placer" and quartz, was carried on at Camp Ferrar, Castle Dome, Eldorado Cañon, and other points; no remuneration was found commensurate with the labor.

In '63 the Vulture mine was located near the present site of Wickenburg. The ledge was very rich in gold, but as the ore had to be hauled twelve miles for reduction, and the expense of transportation of all supplies was so great, the profit was usually on the wrong side of the account. For two years the monthly yield was about thirty-eight thousand dollars, and the total expense of working about forty thousand.

Prescott, the present capital of the Territory, is perhaps the only really desirable place for a residence in the whole country. It is built on a plateau, seven thousand feet above the sea level, and almost entirely surrounded by high mountains. Thus, while raised above the heat of the surrounding desert, it is also sheltered from the sudden changes of temperature incident to that climate.

It is not unusual, in some parts, for a person to ride a great part of the day under a broiling sun, and in intense heat, and finish the day and ensuing night with several inches of snow and cold to match. These sudden changes would seem to indicate an unhealthy climate, but such is not the case. On the contrary, probably no country in the world has less sickness, more especially when we consider the manner of living, and the constant exposure to which those outside of the towns are subjected.

Many people imagine, from the long-continued attempts at subjection, and the certain failure which has hitherto attended all such attempts, that the Apache race is almost unlimited in numbers. But such is far from being the case. All the tribes called Apaches, combined, cannot turn out more than from five to seven thousand warriors; and they are spread over a territory from near the Colorado, on the west and north, to near the Rio Grande, on the east and south. The inaccessibility of their domain is their greatest safeguard. Soldiers and citizens must overcome almost insurmountable difficulties in their raids against this worst of all tribes to have any chance of ultimate success. If the Government could secure the services of Jack Swilling and a thousand men of his selection, the whole race could be soon exterminated, and the "reservation" idea be done away with.

The character of the first settlers would not bear too close an investigation, as at least half of them were the scum of the rebellion, and the greater part of the other half were renegades, horse-thieves, and other kinds of criminals, mixed with enough desperadoes from Mexico to give proper seasoning to the whole lot. Gambling, cutting, and shooting were the principal amusements.

As an agricultural country Arizona can never make any mark in the world, but for mineral wealth it is destined to shine forth the richest and brightest of the possessions of this entire land. Bring in railroads, interest capitalists, and mines will be opened, in comparison with which the wonderfully yielding Comstock will sink into comparative insignificance.

CHAPTER XIX.

MORAL AND INTELLECTUAL OUTLOOK.

> " Culture's hand
> Has scattered verdure o'er the land,
> And smiles and fragrance rule serene
> Where barren wilds usurped the scene."
> —BOWRING.

As imperfect an idea, perhaps more so, is held in the East respecting the moral and intellectual features of the Pacific-Coast life as there is of the physical condition of things. It is supposed by thousands that this is a kind of woe-begone looking country, like somewhat to the wilds of Kentucky in the days of Daniel Boone, and that any quiet hour of day or night, from your own dooryard, ferocious wild beasts may be killed, and that "eternal vigilance" must be kept respecting the Indians, while guns, knives, bolted doors, and barricaded windows must be had to withstand the roving banditti and cut-throats that fill the country. A friend of mine, who has been in this State a few years, received a letter from his mother,—a woman of fine intelligence, by the way, who lives in one of the Eastern States,—requesting that he send her a sprig of sage-brush, of which she had heard so much, "*if he could get it without being in danger of wild beasts or Indians.*" A friend who is now in the East was asked "if there are any school-houses and churches in Nevada and California?" Of course there are thousands who know better, but there are thousands who do not, and it is selfish and uncharitable to laugh at or censure them. How many of the people in general know much regarding the special features of Mexico? How much is known by Californians who have not been there of the moral, social, and intellectual condition of things in Maine or New Hampshire, except what they know by inference or analogy?

California is looked upon by the average citizen of the East as being "an everlasting distance away," and it is associated with the "blood-and-thunder" scenes and spirit that very often predominate in new countries, and that used to rule here, lamentably, till the days of the "vigilance committees."

The ideas held respecting this country are perfectly natural. California got a character during the "gold excitement" that hangs to her, and will for many years to come. Then, are not children taught in their natural-history recitations that the grizzly and cinnamon bears, American lions, catamounts, and what not, are found in abundance in California? Then, is it not taught that the "noble red men," "the savages," are being driven farther and farther west toward the Pacific Ocean? And then it is known that they have been "driven" for so long a time that they certainly are in California, for this State does lie bordering on the ocean right where the Indians are being pushed. Then, were not the Lava Beds, where the late Modoc War was fought, in California and Oregon? and were not those Modocs, from all accounts, a most bloodthirsty and heartless set? And then, were not the Oatman girls captured in Arizona but a short distance from California? and is not the surviving one living in this State to-day?

And then it is known that nearly "every nation under heaven" is represented here, and especially are there great hordes of Chinese scattered all over the West by the tens of thousands, and the late excitement against Chinese immigration has but increased the idea of the dangerous character of that people.

These things always go abroad, and much more that is not true, while the moral and religious and intellectual features are not fully known. And are not many of the journals of this coast responsible for the impressions that have been circulated? Do they not speak disparagingly of the Chinese, and publish as "taking news" any depredations by drunken Indians or bad white men or reckless desperadoes, and at the same time decry and call it "religious fanaticism" when any effort is made to make the people better?

Scurrilous remarks by some journals against church interests and religious revivals, and the bitter hoodlum spirit against the temperance women in the late temperance campaigns and local-option elections, have done more to blacken the moral character of California than anything else in the last five years.

The Pacific Coast, like every other place, is interested in getting the best class of immigration. But the best class of men and women want good society, good morals, good educational facilities, and good church-privileges. And the reason that some localities fill up more rapidly than others is because these privileges can be enjoyed in some places better than in others. Take, for instance, Napa and San José. These are places where not only the natural advantages are very fine, but where educational and religious privileges are superior, and the social and moral character is correspondingly good.

Churches are numerous in California, and generally well supported, all things considered. But in most instances they are numerically weak. It can be said, when taken as a whole, that this is a land of fine churches. And there are not many of these churches but have parsonages, which in most instances are supplied with the various necessary articles of furniture.

There is hardly a mining camp but has its church edifice, and very few places of ever so remote a character but the itinerant minister has found it and established his preaching-place. As a rule, however, churches are slimly attended. I doubt if forty thousand people in the whole State of California are regular attendants at church. This includes all the denominations.

California has a Sunday-law, and in many places it is very respectably observed. But in Nevada, be it said to its disgrace and shame, there is no Sunday-law, and but comparatively little observance of the Sabbath.

In the former State the recklessness of Sabbath-breakings is mainly by the natives and foreigners, as it is in most parts of our country.

California may be said to be a religious State,

but it certainly cannot lay much claim to a deep degree of piety. Representatives are here from all parts of the enlightened and the unenlightened world, and they bring—as absolutely as they bring themselves—their religion. The Chinese have their heathen temples erected in all of the cities and prominent towns, and their devotion to the worship of their gods, in its very earnestness, should make the practical Christianity of this coast blush. The same can be said of all the elements from foreign shores,—they bring and unmistakably manifest their religious tenets. French skepticism and German infidelity and Spanish and Italian devotion to the Romish hierarchy are as pronounced as in their native realms.

Of all places in America the Pacific Coast seems to be the most congenial for infidelity, skepticism, and every phase of spiritualism. Whether climate *can* have any influence on the nervous system, so as to warp or corrupt the lines of religious thought, I am not philosopher enough to pretend to answer. Or whether it is in the moral atmosphere that surrounds every one, the impurity of which naturally tends towards engrafting into the mind falsities, I cannot say. But this one thing is well known, that infidelity, skepticism, atheism, deism, mormonism, spiritualism, free-loveism, and every other ungodly and ruinous ism known to the realm of religion, is to be found here. San Francisco is literally surfeited with ghastly-looking, long-haired spiritualists. "Mediums" are to be found everywhere, and their followers are very numerous.

The tendency seems unmistakable, that if a person get in ill favor with his church, or is expelled, he turns spiritualist. If the moral life has been practically bad, a shadowy armor is secured by turning spiritualist. San Francisco, morally speaking, is the Paris of America. Libertinism is no thickly-clouded secret.

These immoral and so-called religious tenets are met by the church, and they form, humanly speaking, an insurmountable barrier. And some of these ideas that have just been mentioned, in a modified form, anon creep into the realm of orthodoxy. Hence it may be stated frankly that while there are many truly spiritual people,—men and women of faith,—and churches, too, the general spiritual tone of the people is not very high. Nobody is insane enough to claim that it is. We have written more especially of the religious spirit of the Coast than of individual places.

While no place in the State, perhaps, can be found where these elements do not exist, there are localities where there are strong, good church influences, and very few places, as already indicated, where there are not church privileges.

Educational advantages are of a very good order. California lays claim,—whether rightly or not it is not for us to decide,—but she lays claim to the best school laws and regulations of any State in the Union. And her public and charitable institutions are not excelled anywhere. The unfortunate of every class are amply provided for. The blind and deaf and dumb have very commodious institutions, while the insane, of which class there are a very large number, are *very well* provided for. The State has two institutions for this class of persons,—one at Stockton and one at Napa. The latter is one of the finest and most commodious buildings I ever saw.

There is a compulsory educational law in California that compels every person between the years of six and fourteen to attend school. And the classification and range of the branches taught indicate that the standard of education will be very good by and by. I am satisfied that in the leading cities of the State the schools are good, and the methods of instruction are very practical. But I do not believe the schools of the State, taken as a whole, will compare favorably with the schools of the East. Many of the teachers are young and inexperienced. They brag very much on their school law, but a school law does not make a good school, necessarily. The law for the examination of applicants for teacher's license is very strict, but that law very often has illiterate persons to enforce it.

I received a business letter from a teacher who had just been passed by the board of examination "with flying colors," and had a teacher's license for several counties, as well as a State license, who began his letter with "*my dear friend.*" He had evidently not been used to capital letters.

But California has a good law at the foundation of her school system, and this being so, the practical part of the educational machinery will improve as time passes.

One thing that manifests itself in the educational department of the State is a very great fear of seeming to be influenced by anything that bears the impress of moral teaching. In many places the ridiculous and disgraceful act of ruling the Bible out of the schools has been accomplished. Some time ago the school board of San Francisco even prohibited the repetition of the Lord's Prayer, as though that were a sectarian production. Jews, Catholics, Protestants, all classes can join together in saying that prayer, but when it is repeated in the schools it at once becomes sectarian (?). The puzzling question is, to all, which sect is advanced by it. There is a cry raised against any kind of religious act being performed in our public schools, just as though a perfect absence of all moral and religious influence were preferable to religious worship, or that heathenism and infidelity are desirable before religious form.

It is a mistake that our Catholic or Jewish friends, as a body, demand that the Bible shall be thrown out and the Lord's Prayer discarded. They do no such thing, as their leading men affirm. It is simply a truckling to the miserable, low, infidel element in society.

In San Francisco, where the Bible has been put out and the Lord's Prayer forbidden, the desires of the majority, and they the thinking, best class, must be utterly disregarded, and the demands of the minority complied with.

At Berkley the State University is located. There is an attendance, I have learned, of upwards of three hundred students. Here, I have been told, there is not a word of prayer, nor a chapter from the Bible read, at the hour of worship, for they have none. This is said in shame for the great State of California, for it is due her that her character shall not be blackened by the utter disregard of the idea of a God and his word in the education of the young men that must soon rule the destinies of the State.

CHAPTER XX.

LOCALITIES AND BUSINESS.

"The world has nothing to bestow;
From our own selves our joys must flow,
And that dear hut, our HOME."—COTTON.

THE world's gifts are very unevenly distributed. And concerning the cause of this, whether it is in ourselves or is providential, we need not philosophize. The great fact is before us. This is a world of lords and serfs; not legally so, yet none the less real.

The teeming millions of earth are busy, sweating with toil, enduring pains, and burdened with heartaches, all that a morsel of that never-fully-enjoyed something, called *happiness*, might be had. The poor man, the real serf,[1] is dependent often upon the rich, not alone for his own position and livelihood, but the relative happiness of his family flows from the same source.

Tens of thousands of men have but little of the social part of life, while in politics they do not think for themselves; and in religious matters there is little development of the emotional on their own part, or a cultivation of the spiritual, by those who can and should be instructors in such things.

An infinity of distance stretches between men in sympathy, feelings, and love, who move shoulder to shoulder every day. But there is a realm where the iron heel of the despot can, at most, but measurably come, where the heart lays off some of its sorrows, and where a draught of comfort comes to the weary one. Nor does its boon depend on gold or tinsel, or gilded scenery, or richest upholstery, or dizzy whirl of the dance, or flowing wine. It is HOME. No wealth can buy it, and there is no realm like it. "Be it ever so humble, there is no place like home."

The triplet that stands at the head of this chapter has a deal of truth in it. The world doesn't bestow anything. "And from ourselves our joys must flow, and that dear hut, our home," because we make it and them as they are.

"There *is* many a joy in the path of life,
If we would but stop to find it."

But we trample a thousand under our feet in running after those we never reach.

It may be safely said that home, with its attendant ideas, is the ruling power of the American people. The principle betimes may be so warped as hardly to be recognizable, but it exists. And the great question in every mind is, Where can I do the best for myself and family? The world recognizes ambition as a laudable possession, yet there are associations whose treatment of it would indicate that it is entirely illegal, and as such to be punished. But this is only in the minds of a few, hence men go and come without "let or hindrance," that they might advantage themselves and theirs.

As has been said before in this volume, it is a long way to California from the Eastern States, and the change is attended with many inconveniences. I haven't a doubt but that persons with energy and care can do well here; but I would advise any one not to come unless there is some strong reason for it that cannot be overcome in the East.

I can think of but five reasons that can be supposed to induce any one to make the change from the East to extreme West; and these reasons we designate as social, religious, intellectual, financial, and climatic. And it is absurd for any one to suppose they will be bettered in this country by the first three mentioned, and yet they are fair here; but they are at least equally good in the East. Financial opportunities are better here, I am inclined to think. Gold and silver are the money-basis. Yields are great and command a good price. But, then, money is not all. He who thinks so has taken a poor view of life. The greatest boon of California is the climate. But this, while it is the source of a great deal of the enjoyments of life, is *not* all. Besides, there are thousands of persons with whom this climate does not agree. And there are many diseases that it is a positive disadvantage to. And many invalids will be hurried out of the world by coming here, who would live longer in the East. Upon the other hand, many will have a new lease on life by coming to these shores.

Lung disease, if in the first stages, will be benefited, doubtless, but if in the last stages, it will be a great disadvantage. Kidney, uterine, and nervous diseases are not helped; this country is very bad on the latter. By all means do not bring a diseased nervous system to this coast.

We have said this much respecting a change to the Pacific Coast, which should not be made without some well-grounded reason. If it is decided upon, every one should determine before starting what he wants to do after he gets here. Financially, the summer is the best time to come; because, in the fall, about the time the rains begin, business has its greatest change. Especially is this the case in agricultural life. Dwelling-houses can be rented at any time, but it is almost an impossibility to rent a farm, or ranch of any kind, except in the fall. And, after that time, positions and places, as a rule, will be taken.

Farming is not so general here, in many places, as in the East. It is mainly all wheat, or all something else, just as the locality will produce. In the northern part of the State, the valleys are very fine farming land for wheat, grass, and some kinds of fruits. Corn is raised in some places. The great want, be it remembered, is irrigation. If water were plentiful corn could be raised successfully anywhere. The Sacramento valley is very fine for vegetables, wheat, grass, and fruits. It is too far north for oranges, lemons, and such tropical productions. The San Joaquin valley is the great wheat section when it is not affected by drouth, which occurs every few years. Napa, Sanoma, and Petaluma valleys are fine farming sections, and will produce nearly anything.

Irrigation is not essential generally. The coast counties are the locations for potato raising and dairies, neither of which requires a great deal of capital. And at the proper season of the year nearly always there are farms for rent, and some good openings present themselves.

Santa Clara valley, in which San José is located, is among the best places for agricultural pursuits. It is not disturbed with drouth, as San Joaquin valley, nor with damp, cold air, like some northern localities. And yet this valley is sometimes afflicted with comparatively dry weather, as it is this year. The bee-culture is relatively good here, but not so profitable as farther south. My opinion is based upon observation and information that I deem reliable, that the valleys north of the bay are preferable, both as places of residence and as locations, for farming and out-door pursuits.

Monterey County is a fine location for the dairy business; but the affairs of the county, I have learned, are in a serious muddle, and titles to real estate are of such a doubtful and uncertain character that it is not advisable to go there. By all means, in coming to California make sure of what you get. Take nothing for granted but taxation and death.

If fruit-raising be the desire, Southern California is the best place. There the tropical and semi-tropical fruits grow to perfection, and the profits are good. North of Los Angeles oranges do not do so well, because there are either high winds or else it is too cold; and then in Southern California farming can be carried on very successfully. The best of wheat, barley, oats, and corn are raised, frequently without any irrigation.

As already said, San Bernardino County has perhaps the best openings, because land is cheaper. If a man has a small farm, and will cultivate fruit, and raise bees and poultry, he can be sure of a living.

It is hard to give any advice to mechanics, because openings are not very numerous for them. Of course, San Francisco or Sacramento must furnish them the most chances. But the former city is literally overrun, for everybody comes to it. Perhaps, on an average, in the city of San Francisco, there are five applicants for every vacancy that occurs. Yet there are large machine-shops and factories here that must have hands to run them, and hence some will get positions. But the chances are so meagre as hardly to be worth looking after.

As many, perhaps the greater number of persons, come to California in search of health, it is necessary to have an eye on climate as well as business. It has already been indicated what can be done in various parts of the State in many of the business enterprises. But, if possible, it is very desirable to combine a successful and favorite business with a genial and health-producing climate. And of the climate of California it is almost an impossibility to give a correct idea, because every climate of the known world is to be found here, and the distance of but a few miles makes a very great difference in climatic effects. For instance, during the whole year round, Oakland, just east of the bay, has a mild, balmy climate, in which "December is literally as pleasant as May." There are no violent, piercing winds, like there are in San Francisco, barely six miles away. For me, of all climates I have ever seen, San Francisco has the worst. It is precisely in keeping with its moral atmosphere, with immediate church influences left out. You never can tell when to provide yourself with an overcoat. Indeed, you can see overcoats and furs, and lace shawls and light clothing, nearly any time within half a block. As near as I ever came to freezing, I thought, was the last day of July in this city. The warm weather is in the winter; then there is not so much high wind nor heavy fogs. I have never been in this city but that I got sick. The climate does agree, however, with many persons, but it certainly will not with persons predisposed to consumption. The high, cold winds, driving, blinding dust, generally, or the damp, heavy fogs, render the climate very disagreeable, and to many dangerous. But anywhere across the bay, from twenty minutes to an hour's ride, it is wholly different. At Oakland it is balmy, while at San Rafael it is even hot in the summer season. It should be remarked here, that while some of these locations are very warm in the summer and cool in the winter, there is a variation of only eight degrees in San Francisco in the entire year. At Sacramento, Marysville, Stockton, and down the San Joaquin valley, it is very hot, with a decided tendency to malaria.

San José has a delightful climate, except that the nights are very cool, and sometimes damp. The climate here agrees very finely with most people. There is a sharpness about the atmosphere that is bracing. Why it is I have not learned, but physicians say there is a decided tendency to biliousness in very many of the prominent localities of the State.

I have never yet seen a place outside of the mountain districts where there was not, with all the delightful climate, an enervating influence upon nearly every one.

Even at Santa Barbara, where they claim to be the main sanitarium of the entire coast, this is felt. It is said by physicians that consumptives and nervous people should go to the southern part of the State.

Upon the immediate coast anywhere it is not pleasant to anybody, because of the fogs and chilly winds, and yet some very lucrative businesses can be carried on, such as dairying, potato raising, etc., that will compensate for the unpleasantness, if health is not involved.

But, as already stated, nobody can give definite directions or full information concerning the very things alluded to in this chapter. The various features of this country seem to be endless. Every one should know well what they are coming here for, and what they expect to do when they get here, before they start; then it will not be a very difficult matter to determine the location when the journey is completed.

It is perfect folly to come to San Francisco expecting to find a ready opening. Better by far stop in the first mountain-camp that can be found. This city has one-third of the population of the entire State, and of course is absolutely overrun with persons who cannot get employment, because employment cannot be had.

CHAPTER XXI.

SOME OBJECTIONS.

"A mote it is, to trouble the mind's eye."—SHAKSPEARE.

A COMMON-SIZED truth can be told in the East regarding much that is found on the Pacific Coast that will, in an average crowd, be denounced, *in toto*, as an unfounded falsehood. No man ever went from here to the East, and gave anything like a minute description of the country, but what he was charged by some one as "having caught California morals" so badly that his veracity was warped.

One very soon imbibes the spirit of "puffing," because he must give facts, and he cannot do this without seeming to exaggerate. This is not Paradise in any sense; he who has lived here will verify that. And lest the patient reader has concluded that "all *is* gold that glitters," we give this chapter of objections not mixed with the "rosy side of morn."

I am convinced that, in some respects, California has never been exaggerated. The real, pure facts in regard to some things by far exceed the range of reason and credulity; then why think of overstatement? For instance, corn does, once in a while, yield from one hundred and fifty to two hundred bushels per acre; barley one hundred and fifty bushels per acre; and wheat up to a hundred bushels per acre.

Of course, these are exceptions, yet not so unfrequent as one would think, but verily true, O doubting Thomases! A thousand other things are in the same ratio.

The scenery is surpassingly grand; the climate seems to be near perfection; the agricultural products are really enormous; and the mineral wealth no man can compute.

But with all these facts, and more than can be told you, my dear reader, California has its objections,—objections, too, that to many are serious. We may parenthetically say, that for many reasons we do not like this country, while for many reasons we are greatly fascinated by it. What of that? Was there ever a country on earth whose main characteristic was perfection? How foolish to think so!

We look through our individual glasses, and are affected just in proportion as the lenses are adapted to the object; so, as it regards this or any other country, a man is interested just in proportion as the adaptedness is perfect between himself and the country. Hence no one can or ought to pass sentence upon California, or any other place, for everybody else, without giving his reasons.

I state it as a general rule, that while I know more money can be made here than in the East, *the masses* should consider but one cause for coming to this State, for at present the masses of people are not adapted to California life and business. The one reason alluded to is health. And then the invalid should ascertain if the disease is of such a character that this climate will affect it for the better.

A person might come here for climatic effect upon organic heart disease, and of course failing, as he must, would go back denouncing this country as the most ponderous fraud of the universe; while a person predisposed to consumption would hail this as the long-sought-for Eldorado.

It is just so in business, the professions, or social life. If the hog-dealer were to move to California, expecting to carry on a very extensive speculation in hogs, or the associate article, corn, he would pronounce the Golden State to be nothing less than a golden humbug.

But the wheat-merchant would say that this is his commercial heaven.

If the physician, yearning for the delights of this State, and yet having an eye or two on quinine, cerebro-spinal meningitis, chills, anti-malarious nostrums, etc., were to come here, he would think this State an unparalleled swindle, for he would seldom find these diseases, or have little need of his Peruvian barks as a general thing. But we are half-way premeditating, without stating the objections.

The alkali and the various kinds of soil are often serious objections. That would seem to the reader to be an absurdity, yet such is the fact, for there is often the most beautiful superficial appearance to the landscape, with a black, rich-looking soil, yet mixed with it may be a fearful amount of alkali,—a native form of potash,—that ruins the land. Or it may be "doby,"—that is, a thick, mucky, pasty soil, that is exceedingly rich, yet very hard to manage, and the very kind that would deceive any one inexperienced in that kind of lands.

Land titles are frequently of a fearful character. Of course there are many that have been sifted, and are perfectly good, yet the difficult question to answer is, "which is which?"

This bad-title disease is often like the milk sickness was years ago in the State of Illinois, always in some other locality than the one you chance to be in. But this is more frequently among the natives than those who have immigrated to this State. And it only requires a business care in any locality to be perfectly safe.

The lack of manufactories is another objection frequently offered, and not without foundation. At present there are few other than woollen factories and flouring mills. It must be remembered that factories spring up in accordance to the demands, and these mentioned are those in the greatest demand. Besides, this is a new State; but, notwithstanding that, she cannot but feel proud of her enterprise and productions.

Hitherto a want of railroads has been a serious objection, but that is being remedied, and, no doubt, in a few years every part of the State will be quite accessible by this means of travel. The State has now a main line running from the east to San Francisco, and an arm running northward toward Oregon, while the southern part of the State, the garden of it all, is reached by a line of railroad. At the close of last year there were one thousand eight hundred and fifty-four miles of railroad being operated in California.

The new-comer almost invariably raises an objection to the elements of social life. Everything is so different from what he has been accustomed to. The ordinary rules that govern many features of social life in the East are here wholly different.

More of the real heart is seen here,—more frankness, *pro* and *con*, which at first is taken for brusqueness, and sometimes is. Stoicism and frigid selfishness are not so dominant here as one at first supposes. Outside the lines of certain formalities you cannot find a more liberal people,—too liberal. The old benevolent instincts of the earlier immigrants still adhere to the people. For worthy purposes they are very liberal.

The excitement and hurly-burly of this whole coast is really unpalatable to one accustomed to different ways of life. Excitement in semi-homœopathic doses is relished by most of us, but when it floods all departments of society it gets to be surfeiting.

A gentleman once said to me, "Everybody, from the hod-carrier to the millionaire, is excited here." It was an honest confession, and doubtless a fact, for a residence of three years on the Coast has shown us that there is one continuous spirit of excitement, but it is no great adornment to California life. There are more suicides and cases of insanity here than in any other State in the Union.

The moral and religious status of society in general is objectionable to one from the warm religious fervor of the East. Persons feel this more than all else beside, at first. And yet society is good, in the general acceptation of the term. But the moral sense has moved in a different chan-

L.*

nel, while the religious fervor has not been greatly developed.

As a rule, church membership is small even in large towns. Churches, and in some instances ministers, have not a very strong hold on the community at large. This may not be any fault of society. Vast areas of the country that are thickly settled, while they have ample school facilities, have few or no churches. Many of the California people do not lay much emphasis on church-going, and yet churches are well supported pecuniarily. Spirituality is in many localities very meagre, and the formality very painful.

Perhaps the three first and greatest objections raised to the Pacific Coast by those desiring to come, or those having arrived very recently, are to the winds, dust, and probable earthquakes.

These objections, at the distance of many hundreds and thousands of miles, really seem to be very formidable. For no one desires to be blinded with dust, or buried in a sand-bank in a night, or blown out of the country, or have his house blown to atoms about his head, or face the indescribable terrors of an earthquake. These very ideas are entertained by many who have not learned better by experiencing the reality.

There are high winds occasionally. In some localities they last about three days,—seldom more, oftener less. And of course these winds are generally accompanied with more or less dust. But what of it? All the winds and dust in a twelvemonth do not entail as much anxiety and inconvenience as *one* of the severe storms that visit the East in the summer. And as it regards earthquakes, all that will probably come in five years will not equal in destruction one Eastern tornado.

It is said that there have been but *five* persons killed by earthquakes in California since 1848.

The dread of this phenomenon is superficial, for most persons after being here awhile have a desire to experience one. But this desire is also short-lived, for one earthquake usually satisfies the most curious. These objections, as many I have mentioned, like the mirages that often attract on the plains, are not on close examination very real.

This is a land of monopolies. Everything from a silver mine to a bootblack is monopolized. You will find this out as soon as you arrive. There are two great parties regarding everything,—the "ins" and the "outs." Turns sometimes come when relative places are changed, but it requires a large degree of pressure and labor.

A prominent lawyer once said to me, "The questions asked here of a new-comer are, 'How much money has he? How can it be gotten the easiest?'" This remark, doubtless, was a little colored, but it contains a shadow of truth in it.

Going into business, you must look well to the

surroundings and the extent of the systematic monopoly that is already held of the very business you may desire to enter.

We have said that there is good society, in the absolute sense of the term. So there is. But there is a gilded edge to society, frequently, that allures and fascinates, but beneath it is full of rottenness. No part of our great country has a more refined immorality than the Pacific Coast, and in no part is the moral sentiment lower, with tens of thousands, than here. It is, in my mind, the greatest objection to California. In many parts, it is a lamentable misfortune that families should be raised amidst the moral pollution that now exists. I would most unhesitatingly advise a man having a family to raise, unless he can locate in one of the few places where the morals of the society are good, to remain in the East.

No attention, as a rule, should be given to colonization societies or land companies. It may be stated as a general rule that men are not going to greatly interest themselves in getting persons from the East here without a fine profit accruing to themselves for their trouble, notwithstanding their favorable advertising. Thousands have been drawn here by persons calling themselves colonization societies and landed companies, who have not enough left, after getting here, to get back upon, and not enough to live upon here. Sometimes it is better to ".go it blind" than to be caught, as there is danger of being, by professional land-hucksters. It is often dangerous to trust a friend.

CHAPTER XXII.

MY ASSOCIATE.

"The amity that wisdom knits not, folly may easily untie."—SHAKSPEARE.

"Weak though we are, to love is no hard task,
And love for love is all that Heaven does ask."
—WALLER.

WE plan, but God disposes. How little we know when we begin a task who shall end it, or, in fact, whether it shall be ended at all!

We are governed largely by the influence of association. It is an old saying, long ago adjudged true, that "as iron sharpeneth iron, so a man sharpeneth the countenance of his friend." Associations are not always formed because of the liabilities that may be laid upon the partnership, but often because of the inspiration that comes through the force of association. "BEYOND THE SIERRAS" would have been a storehouse of richer fruit to the reader had it been untrue that

"Death loves a shining mark."

"The Great West," as it was known and written of a score of years ago, has lost its frontier characteristics in the insuperable drive and rush of business and the advance of civilization. The Rocky Mountains join hands with the Atlantic Ocean, and between the two the word "frontier" has no longer a meaning as it once had.

California, the American Italy, flings back the appellation of "frontier," but holds to the charge of being a new and wondrous country. Such it is recognized, and to it thousands of eyes are being turned. How eagerly is information sought by those desiring to find the new Eldorado! and how comparatively little they get, they too well know.

To give this as reliably as we could, that those emigrating might not be burdened with regrets because of a total lack of information, has been our design. A little only has been given; it is like studying the preface of a book while the volume lies beyond, for to know this country one must be here. These mountains must be climbed, these cañons explored, these fertile valleys seen, and the inspiration of these incomparable wonders felt, to know this country.

The sense in which we have just used the pronoun is not that that prompts the editor in his work, but in a literal meaning; for there started with me in the preparation of this volume one whose long residence on the Pacific Coast eminently fitted him to know well of the country, and whose literary ability qualified him to impart information to others. His hand penned a few of these pages, and then stiffened in death. Hon. Wirt Hopkins was one of those rare men that makes an associate in the most absolute sense of the term. He evidenced the truth of the couplet,—

> "Friendship's the wine of life, but friendship new
> Is neither strong nor pure."

For time, instead of weakening, as is too often the case, strengthened the fraternal feelings of his life. There are some men whose whole natures are superficial. You can no more depend upon their friendship than you can upon their word.

The definition of a gentleman given to me once, that "a friend is one who treats you friendly," may be as far from correct as the "east is from the west." Since the memorable time when the "Hail, Master!" and the kiss, were the deceitful steps to the betrayal of our Lord, it must not be taken for granted that a man is a friend because he *simply* treats you as such.

Be it said to the shame and confusion of some natures at least, that I have seen men surrounded by all the sacredness and solemnity that human imagination could contrive, kneeling at the altar, with the hands resting on the Bible, one of the greatest "lights" that shines upon the darkened understanding, taking part in a ceremony whose seriousness were enough to move a savage, if he could but understand it. I have seen men under such circumstances, and in such positions, declare there was no one in the assembled number whom they could not forgive, love, and affiliate with. And yet they would arise from the altar, rub shoulder to shoulder with some of their "brethren," look into their eyes, mix in the "mystic associations" of the sacred scene, and never exchange the slightest fraternal greeting, bitter enemies still.

It is refreshing, and gives us a better view of human nature, to meet and be associated with men who, without the force of "obligation," so-called, and ceremony, are true as the needle to the pole. Such a man was Mr. Hopkins, my lamented friend, who associated with me for the formation of this volume. But he was hardly permitted to fully begin the work before death clipped the thread, and stopped the loom of life.

Hon. Wirt Hopkins, A.M., was born in West Groton, Tompkins County, New York, February 15, 1834. When he was but a year old he was attacked with asthma, from which he was always a great sufferer, except when in certain localities of very pure or rarefied air. He was a descendant of the celebrated Presbyterian divine, Rev. Samuel Hopkins, D.D., of anti-slavery notoriety, from whom he seemed to inherit his acuteness of thought and his analytical mind.

His intellectual mould was of the rarest kind, and his mind was well disciplined by education. Although a sickly, delicate child, he began the study of classic literature when he was but four years of age; and when he was but eight years old he read such works as Virgil, Homer, Xenophon's Anabasis, the Memorabilia, etc., as a mere pastime.

At the age of twelve or thirteen, on account of his extreme suffering from asthma, he was sent South, where it was hoped he would be benefited by a milder climate, and could be further educated. He became a student at Transylvania University, under the celebrated Dr. Bascom, afterward bishop. Here, and when he was not more than fourteen years of age, he corrected the manuscript for Dodd's Arithmetic, that was afterward used very generally in the common schools of the Middle States.

His ill health made it necessary for a change to the Pacific Coast, which was made in 1853. Since that time Mr. Hopkins rummaged through almost every nook and corner of the Pacific States and the Sandwich Islands, all to regain his health. Like an old-time Pacific coaster that he was, he had the faculty of adapting himself to circumstances. In this feature his was a fine representation of California life. When he died, March 24,

1877, he was, and had been for a number of years, filling, the position of Assayer of the United States Mint.

His life closed as calmly and as peacefully as sinks the sun at eventide behind his mountain home. The same clear mind that characterized him all through life lasted till his spirit was kissed away to God. The declaration of his dying hour was, "Christianity is the foundation of the world."

Association is one of Nature's foremost laws; kindredship is not so prominent. We deal with some men, mingle with them, live very near them, so that we are intimately associated with them, but with their spirits we feel not the slightest kindredship. Then there are men whose lives seem to mingle and flow on with our own,—there is a kindred feeling in every department of the mind. The intimacy is like that of David and Jonathan, ever strengthening and sweetening as the years roll by. When they are gone, we feel that a part of ourselves is taken away. And the isolation of life, that anon is felt, is understood as it cannot be under any other circumstances.

Associated, pleasant work, that filled hands and heart and brain, bound myself and my departed friend very closely together. Seldom do I get so near men, seldom do men get so near me, as we were to each other. His mind, well filled with classic literature and history and science and poetry, and his childish simplicity, were the magnets that drew me near him. He made me a stronger man, while, by the help of God, I made him a better man. Among his last words to me, as life ebbed away, were, "Of all men you are the first that fixed my mind on Christ." As I pen these lines that beautiful poem of Moore's comes trooping up, that contains the verse,—

> "When I remember all
>   The friends, so linked together,
> I've seen around me fall,
>   Like leaves in wintry weather;
> I feel like one who treads alone
>   Some banquet-hall deserted,
> Whose lights are fled, whose garland's dead,
>   And all but he departed."

This sad refrain of the poet will find an echo in thousands of hearts that have been cheered by the benefactions of my friend. And nobler impulses will be set in motion, and bright memories of the past awakened, as tracing these lines they shall associate him with scenes BEYOND THE SIERRAS.

THE END.

www.ingramcontent.com/pod-product-compliance
Lightning Source LLC
Chambersburg PA
CBHW031948230426
43672CB00010B/2090